Endorsements

"Another remarkable contribution from the prolific pen of Jon Zens."

–Frank Viola, author of *God's Favorite Place*
on Earth **and** *From Eternity to Here*

"Jon has done something which is very difficult to do. He has written a concise book on the nature and life of the *ekklesia* of Jesus Christ. In the pages of *Jesus Is Family*, Jon has succeeded in putting together a wonderful, biblical, and spiritually accurate description of the Family, Body, House, and Community of God in Christ. I personally have waited a long time for a reference like this! Now, when believers ask me for a short book on what we believe and practice about the *ekklesia*, I can give them a copy of this book. Thanks Jon!"

–Milt Rodriguez, author of *The Community*
Life of God **and** *The Temple Within*

"I recommend *Jesus Is Family* without hesitation to any believer or Christian fellowship committed to or interested in the New Testament alternative to institutional church. It serves also as an excellent tool for reflection for those who are already gathering together as family in Christ, clearly identifying the essential marks of an "organic" assembly of Jesus-loving people for whom Christ alone is the one and only Lead Pastor. This book is so helpful in highlighting the spectrum of colors in the Light of our Lord's Body and Bride that is to irradiate into the world from His indwelling of us who love Him sir

–Dennis J. Mulkey, Ph.D., aut

D1075950

"With *Jesus Is Family: His Life Together*, Jon brings his sharp eye for historical detail into view and opens a creaky window—one that's been long painted shut by numerous layers institutional necessity—to let the glorious Light of Day in. And, in true Zens form and style, readers can count on clear, reasoned dialogue and savor the joy of his practical simplicity. Hurting hearts, or those especially disappointed by a corporation-style, consumerist version of Christianity will be encouraged to hear words that refresh the soul. By reminding us that one of the foundational metaphors of Christ's Body is family, Jon brings the reader back to the basics of meaningful life in the gathering of God's people. From celebration, remembering, and listening, to faith, healing, and genuine caring for others as brothers and sisters, Jon brings all the elements necessary for Christ-centered community to a hungry, thirsty, brood of 21st century believers. Thank you, brother. Thank you, kindly."

–Stephanie Bennett, PhD., Professor of Communication and Media Ecology and author of *Within the Walls* trilogy and *Communicating Love: Staying Close in a 24/7 Media-Saturated Society*

"Packed with arresting quotes and valuable references, and rich with original insights, *Jesus Is Family* is an easy-to-read, user-friendly crash course in church-life. Defying convention without violating Scripture, Jon convincingly argues that an authentic spiritual community, rooted in hospitality and allowing its members true freedom in Christ, is the surest incubator for genuine spiritual growth. If you're longing to escape the "closed space" of institutional church and enter the "open space" of truly biblical community, *Jesus Is Family* is the much-needed key to unlocking that door."

–Richard Jacobson, Author of *Unchurching: Christianity Without Churchianity*

Jesus is Family

His Life Together

JON ZENS

OTHER BOOKS BY THE AUTHOR

- *A Church Building Every 1/2 Mile: What Makes American Christianity Tick?*

- *What's With Paul & Women? Unlocking the Cultural Background to 1 Timothy 2*

- *No Will of My Own: How Patriarchy Smothers Female Dignity & Personhood*

- *Christ Minimized? A Response to Rob Bell's Love Wins*

- *The Pastor Has No Clothes: Moving from Clergy-Centered Church to Christ-Centered Ekklesia*

- *To Preach or Not to Preach? The Church's Urgent Question* (David C. Norrington with Replies to the Critics & an Introduction by Jon Zens)

- *58 to 0: How Christ Leads Through the One Anothers*

Available online at: www.JonZens.com

Dedication

This book is dedicated to Tim Buss whose love and expression of Christ has affected me deeply.

Copyright © 2017 by Jon Zens.

First Edition

Cover artwork: "Poppies" by Dotty Zens
Cover design and layout: Rafael Polendo (polendo.net)

Unless otherwise identified, all Scripture quotations in this publication are taken from the Holy Bible, New International Version®, NIV®. Copyright ©1973, 1978, 1984, 2011 by Biblica, Inc.™ Used by permission of Zondervan. All rights reserved worldwide. www.zondervan.com The "NIV" and "New International Version" are trademarks registered in the United States Patent and Trademark Office by Biblica, Inc.™

ESV Bible® (The Holy Bible, *English Standard Version*®), copyright © 2001 by Crossway Bibles, a publishing ministry of Good News Publishers. Used by permission. All rights reserved. www.crossway.org.

ISBN 978-1-938480-23-2

This volume is printed on acid free paper and meets ANSI Z39.48 standards.

Printed in the United States of America

 QUOIR

Published by Quoir
Orange, California

www.quoir.com

Table of Contents

Foreword by Skeeter Wilson 9

Opening Comments 11

Setting the Stage 13

1. Family Is In Our Hearts 15

2. Family Is the Lord's Heart 19

3. Family Gathers...At Home 23

4. Family Is Hospitality 27

5. Family Is *Ekklesia* 31

6. Family Is Freedom 37

7. Family Is Safe 43

8. Family Is...Imperfect 49

9. Family Meats Together 53

10. Family Meets Together 59

11. Family Celebrates Together 65

12. Family Is Relational 69

13. Family Cares for One Another 75

14. Family Is Healing 81

15. Family Is Led 85

16. Family Is "Adam" 89

17. Jesus Is Family 93

For Further Reflection 99

Appendix: A.W. Tozer's Final Words in 1963 101

Foreword

It was forty years ago that I first met Jon Zens. At the time we met I was a part of an institutional church that was in crisis. Jon was invited along with others to help moderate the issues that were fracturing our gathering of believers. I became increasingly aware over the years that at stake was a struggle between the long history of tradition that defines modern Christianity and a radical return to a faith that rests in Christ alone.

Long before we met, both Jon and I, in our own ways, were battling with the piles of baggage and presuppositions that have become virtually synonymous with modern expressions of Christianity.

I don't presume to speak for Jon on this, but it seems throughout my walk with Christ, the moment I discovered and discarded one item of historical baggage, a dozen more surfaced that cried to be addressed. Certainly, the battle to recapture the centrality of the Person and work of Christ, alone, has been as much an internal struggle with my own preconceptions as it has been with those outside forces that do not want to give up their "ways."

I have taken some comfort in the fact that most of the New Covenant epistles were written to thwart the false teachings and traditions that were in one sense or another a "false gospel." But there are some books, perhaps *Hebrews* is a prime example, that were written with a different approach. It battled false ideas, but it did so by positing a *positive premise*, "but in these last days He has spoken to us by His Son," and then demonstrated throughout the book the primacy of the Son.

As I read *Jesus Is Family*, I was struck by the idea that here is Jon's version of the *positive premise* that *Christ Is Family*. It is worth remembering that the battles against deeply embedded traditions are worth the fight, because they stand in the way of something infinitely better—Christ alone. And with the encumbrances set aside, we stand related as the family of Christ, a phenomenon of God. The restoration of all things is summed up in the event of family; a family restored with Christ unto and into the eternal realms.

It is a good thing to explore the *positive premise* that Jon postulates. Our Lord spoke against religion, tradition, and self-righteousness, but he offered life in a new family, "For whoever does the will of My Father who is in heaven, he is My brother and sister and mother." Herein is the postulate that describes who our Christ is: He is family.

–Skeeter Wilson, Author of *Worthless People* and *Crossing Rivers,*
two-time graduate of the University of Alaska-Anchorage.

Opening Comments

In August of 2014 a gathering was held in Garden Grove, California, called "Infusion." I presented "Christ on Earth as Community" at one of the sessions. In the months prior to this conference, as I read and meditated, the Lord was putting "community" on my heart. After returning from Garden Grove, I felt like these perspectives should perhaps become a book. I shared the skeletal thoughts of this presentation with a person I respected, and they said, "You are onto something great here, Jon. It's going to be a lot of work, but it will dwell in the heart of our Father!" I cannot speak to the first and third parts of this statement, but I can say that the second part was very accurate— it was a lot of work. Not in the sense that it was laborious, for it flowed naturally for the most part, but in the sense that many concepts were difficult to put into words. The reason for this may be that such dimensions of the Lord's house must come by the Spirit taking the words on a page and bringing *revelation from Christ* to human hearts.

I began the manuscript in the first week of December, 2016, and it was completed on March 14, 2017. It was then sent to a number of brothers and sisters with the request for feedback. What I have received back has been extremely helpful in sharpening the manuscript. In this light, I want to give a hearty "thanks" to Jim Judkins, Mark Lake, Dennis Mulkey, Arlan Purdy, Mary Ellen Robinson, Marv and Jodi Root, Catherine Seebald, and Charlene Wilder for the hard work they put into their suggested edits.

I can only pray that my feeble, stammering words will be used by the Lord to encourage others to express affection to

Christ in the heavenlies, to let Christ in them flow like a river, and to function with Jesus on earth—in His *ekklesia*.

Setting the Stage

Obviously, peoples' experience in churches varies and has many nuances, but there are certain patterns that parallel what many have gone through. I believe the following brief story by a dear sister will resonate with many who have felt compelled to leave local churches. For our purposes here, please note the theme of *family* that emerges. At the outset, the feeling of family was strong in the new group. Then, with the acquisition of a pastor and building, the family atmosphere disappeared. Later in time, this sister longed for the early days when they were smaller and more like a family. Here is her narrative:

> A bit of background. I left an Institutional Church just nine months ago. I have gone to church my entire life (was a PK) and have always been heavily involved in church. Eighteen years ago, a number of people (including myself) left a denominational church over a serious issue of doctrine. After meeting in our basement for a few weeks and discussing what we were going to do, we realized we were already a "church" and so we started a new one. (Our first mistake…hindsight is 20/20!) Things were great for a while. We were like a family and there was a lot of love and encouragement and support. But over time we hired a pastor, bought a building and grew in numbers. By most standards, we were still a small congregation (highest average attendance of about 180) but still one of the biggest churches in our small town of several thousand people. I often felt like the church was my "child" that I had helped give birth to. It was a huge part of my life and I felt responsible for how things turned out. Anyway, without going into all the details, there were many things that happened over the years that just struck me as "wrong" and "not how a church should operate." I'm not blaming anyone. Since I've left, I see how I also was in error in many ways myself. I reached a point where there was an incident that occurred that was kind of the "straw that broke the

camel's back" and I checked out mentally and emotionally. It was so glaringly obvious that the sense of community was gone. The relationships had become all about keeping the church functioning and not about caring for each other. I continued to attend for well over a year (mostly because my husband did not want to leave) but reached a point where I just couldn't make myself go any longer. My husband still attends. There have been just a few people who have reached out to me. I've given a few vague (but honest) answers as to why I'm no longer attending. "Church has become more of a negative than a positive in my life right now." "I need some time to just listen to Jesus speak to me without all of the other voices distracting me." And more recently I told someone, "I miss the days when we were smaller and more like a family." All true, but doesn't really get to the heart of the matter. I really believe the people still attending are good people with good hearts. They want to see people come to know Christ and grow in relationship with Him. They've just bought into the kool-aid that the right leadership and programming will make that happen. I should add that we had the same pastor for fifteen years. He resigned and they were without a pastor for a little over a year. The new pastor has only been there for about a year and a half. So he doesn't really know me very well. But I can see how the people of the church are hopeful that he can help the church. He shines in areas where the former pastor was weak. He is doing all the "right things" that they teach in seminary and that you read about on all the websites. But it doesn't really change the core problem (Facebook, March 29, 2017).

This brief narrative, I believe, captures the heart-break and frustration that so many have been through. It highlights the common elements that mark the road from fresh life in the beginning to institutionalism in the end. In the chapters that follow, the importance of Jesus' family, the challenges to it, and the blessings that flow out of it will be unpacked.

CHAPTER 1
Family Is in Our Hearts

"God sets the lonely in families."

—Psalm 68:6

One of the most obvious malaises in our world is the deep sense of loneliness that burdens the multitudes. "There are many, many people," Carl Rogers noted, "living in private dungeons today, people who give no evidence of it whatsoever on the outside, where you have to listen very sharply to hear faint messages from the dungeon." Henri Nouwen observed that "children, adolescents, adults and old people are in growing degree exposed to the contagious disease of loneliness."

Isn't it fascinating that a state of loneliness became the springboard for shedding light on the eternal purpose in Christ? The Lord put Adam in the Garden, and then announced, "It is not good for Adam to be alone; I will make for him a helper comparable to him." Then after Adam had named the animals, it was clear there was no *companion* for him. The Lord, then, made Eve out of Adam. The solution to Adam's *aloneness* was to be one-flesh with *another*, and this opened up the whole purpose of God to secure a Bride for His Son. The Genesis 2 narrative is not ultimately about human marriage, but, as Paul underscored, it is a graphic picture of "a great mystery concerning Christ and the *ekklesia*."

Why is it that humans in the deepest recesses of their being desire to "be with others"? It is because they are created by

Father, Son and Spirit—a *fellowship* of three, yet one. "More and more people are becoming conscious that our God is *family*. Our God is three persons in love with each other; our God is communion" (Jean Vanier). The human longing to "be with" can be suppressed, denied, perverted, or exist as a nagging, unsatisfied feeling. But a *communal sense* is embedded in the very core of humanness.

REALITY IS RELATIONAL TO ITS CORE

The truth is that we were created in Their image to "belong" with others. First of all, of course, is belonging in saving relationship with Him in the *vertical* dimension, but integrally connected to and flowing out of this is the *horizontal* dimension of belonging. John Eldredge has captured some crucial perspectives that easily get lost in the shuffle of life.

"How wonderful to discover that God has never been alone. He has always been Father, Son and Spirit. God has always been a fellowship. The whole story began with something relational... Reality is relational to its core. Whatever else it means to be human, we know beyond doubt that it means to be relational... One of the deepest of all human longings is the longing to belong, to be a part of things, to be invited in...We are relational to the core...From this [Triune] Fellowship spring all our longings for a friend, a family, a fellowship—for someplace to belong" (*Epic*, pp. 20, 22-24).

Tragically, sin has disrupted and misdirected the human desire for "being a part of." It all started with Adam and Eve, and continued on among males and females, families and societies. As the 1980 song put it, people are "lookin' for love in all the wrong places; lookin' for love in too many faces."

The biblical narrative unveils clearly identifiable threads that come to fruition in Christ's appearance in history. The Lord's eternal purpose in Jesus secures redemption from sin and a new family. As Frank Viola put it so well:

> "The triune God is chiefly occupied with…a house and a family for God the Father…a bride and a body for God the Son…the Spirit shares the house, the family, the bride, and the body along with the Father and the Son…The Father obtains a bride for the Son by the Spirit. He then builds a house in which He, the Son, and the bride dwell together in the Spirit. The Father, the Son and the bride live in that house as an extended household and they have offspring by the Spirit. The offspring constitutes a new humanity called 'the body of Christ'" (*From Eternity to Here*, pp. 18-19).

In the journey that unfolds in the following chapters, I will seek to pull the curtain back on vital dimensions of what it means for us to function as *the Lord's family on earth*.

CHAPTER 2

Family Is the Lord's Heart

"According to the Apostle Paul. God is working out His ancient plan in order to have a large family of many sons and daughters all conformed to the character and likeness of His special Son."

–David J. Schonberg

Most of you have heard people say, "Find out what God is doing, and get involved with it." But folks who say this usually have not reflected on the fact that Jesus has already clearly declared His heart and His purpose when He told the disciples, "I will build My *ekklesia*…" The real question is, are we in step with what He has said He will do and is doing?

Interestingly, the verb Jesus used, *oikodomeo,* literally means "to build a house" (*oikos,* "a house," *domeo,* "to build"), hence, to build anything. But in this case the verb reveals the truth—*Jesus is building His house, His family.* He called His family *ekklesia,* which means congregation or assembly. We will unpack the reality of *ekklesia* later, but right now we need to catch a glimpse of the radical way that Jesus defined *family.*

The Jewish culture in Jesus' day was extremely focused on a person's physical family. Everything was built around one's family tree, one's genealogy. The huge no-no, to be avoided at all costs, was to bring *shame* upon the family name.

Jesus, a Jew Himself, shattered the notion that everything vital hinged on your physical lineage. He drew a line in the sand which defined family *as those in relationship to Him, the Messiah.*

This was a *relational*, not physical definition of family. On one occasion, Jesus made this crystal clear:

"While He talked to the crowds, behold His mother and brothers stood outside wishing to speak with Him. Someone said to Him 'Your mother and brothers are outside desiring to speak with You. He answered, 'Who is my mother? Who are My brothers?' And He stretched out His hand toward His disciples and announced, 'Behold, My mother and brothers!—whoever does the will of God is my brother, sister and mother'" (Matt. 12:47-50; Mark 3:34-35).

At other times, Jesus uttered remarks that would leave His Jewish listeners incredulous:

"Brother will deliver up brother to death, and the father the child, and the children will rise up against their parents and put them to death" (Matt. 10:21; Mark 13:12).

"One's enemies will be those in their own family" (Matt. 10:34-36).

First century Judaism was fixated on pedigree, who mom and dad were, and your family line. Into this religious world Jesus brought a Kingdom where something like Ancestry.com was useless and out of place. Except for people like Anna and Simeon, the Jewish population prided themselves in being "Moses' disciples," with Abraham as their father.

In Jesus' realm, however, "as many as received Him, to those He gave the right to become children of God, to those who believe in His name: who were born, not of blood, nor of the will of the flesh, nor of the human will, but of God." Jesus ushered in a "new humanity" where belonging had nothing to do with who your dad was, but all to do with knowing Christ and His "Abba."

Paul affirmed that in Jesus' family all who are Christ's are Abraham's seed, and heirs according to the promise. The "Israel of God" was no longer defined geographically and genealogically, but was defined in Christ as a "new creation," and thus included Gentile believers like the Galatians (Gal. 6:16).

The most basic image used to portray Christ's people is as a *house*, a *family*. Paul told the Corinthians, "you are God's house." Peter told the dispersed believers, "you are living stones in a spiritual home." In the next chapter we will explore some foundational issues concerning the body of Christ as family.

CHAPTER 3
Family Gathers...At Home

After the disciples confessed Him as "the Christ, the Son of the Living God," Jesus promised to build Himself a home called *ekklesia*. The twelve had no idea what this home would look like, or what shape it would take. When Jesus came on the Day of Pentecost in the Spirit, a pattern immediately emerged after people believed and were baptized.

"So continuing daily with one accord in the temple, and breaking bread from home to home, they ate their food with gladness and simplicity of heart."

"And daily in the temple, and in every home, they did not stop teaching and proclaiming Jesus as the Christ."

"As for Saul, he made havoc of the *ekklesia*, entering every home, and dragging off men and women, committing them to prison."

"So, after some reflection, he came to the home of Mary, the mother of John Mark, where many were gathered together praying."

"I taught you publicly and from home to home."

"We who were Paul's companions left and came to Caesarea, and entered the home of Philip the evangelist, one of the seven, and stayed with him. Now this man had four virgin daughters who prophesied."

"Greet Priscilla and Aquila, my fellow workers in Christ Jesus…Likewise greet the *ekklesia* that is in their home."

"Aquila and Priscilla greet you heartily in the Lord, with the *ekklesia* that is in their home."

"Greet the brethren who are in Laodicea, and Nymphas and the *ekklesia* that is in her home."

"To the beloved Apphia, Archippus our fellow soldier, and to the *ekklesia* in your home."

Jesus announced that He would build Himself a home, an *ekklesia*, and that the gates of death would not prevail against it. We can see from the New Testament passages cited above that Christ's *ekklesia* came to fruition primarily in *homes*. There was no compulsion, necessity or mandate to construct a separate *place* "to go" and gather around the Lord.

It is difficult for us to realize what a radical practice this was. The hallmark of all religions, including Judaism, was the presence of a *specially marked off and constructed place for devotees to carry out their rituals*. The early Jesus people had no such buildings. Osiek and Balch capture the ethos of the first century home-based beginnings, and the later developments that destroyed the family atmosphere.

> "While the most luxurious houses offered a certain gracious living, the vast majority of residents of an ancient Mediterranean city or town lived lives full of hardship, poor health, and crowding, with high rates of infant mortality and low life expectancy. In this environment, earliest Christianity was born and developed. All evidence points to domestic buildings [houses] as the first sites for Christian gatherings. Even during the life of Jesus, the house seems to have been a favorite site for teaching…The first groups of his followers after his death began meeting in private houses…In these earliest years, perhaps for the first century and a half, there were probably no structural adaptations for Christian worship, but rather, the adaptation of the group to the structures available…When the group became too large, another was founded in another location…This first phase of Christian worship lasted until the middle or end of the second century, by which time numbers had grown considerably and liturgy was evolving beyond the capacity of domestic architecture to support it. No longer was the Eucharist celebrated at a

common meal, but at a ritual commemoration that retained only the stylized structure of a meal…By this time, houses used as gathering places for Christian assemblies began to be remodeled into buildings better adapted for assembly and worship… Thus what was once a private house became a building devoted to Christian religious use…The separation of the Eucharist from a meal and the growing numbers of believers necessitated the removal of worship from the venue of the private dwelling, and thus *from the family setting*. From then on, Christian worship was conducted according to the profile of public liturgy and *no longer took place in a family environment*. The growing authority of the bishop concentrated more and more powers in the hands, not of local leaders, but of centralized authority figures responsible for larger and larger groups of believers" (*Families in the New Testament World*, pp. 32-35).

What began as a Spirit-driven *family environment* morphed into a *leader-driven*, increasingly institutional, bureaucracy. As Wolfgang Forell rightly observed:

"Yet the institution most effective in containing the threats to the unity of the nascent Christian movement was the gradually evolving office of the bishop. Ethical guidance for people recently converted to Christianity, and likely to bring a pervasive pagan attitude to this new life, *was offered at first by a polyform ministry of grace, reflected in the New Testament*. But as time went by moral authority was increasingly focused in an ordered ministry of bishops and deacons." (George Wolfgang Forell, *History of Christian Ethics*, Vol 1, pages 39-40.)

The "polyform ministry of grace" was expressed by Christ's family pursuing the *58 one another's* in their shared life together. The shift to leader-centeredness put a fatal damper on organic life together.

In underscoring that Jesus' initial *ekklesia*-building was home-based, I want to clarify a few issues. In light of the Savior's conversation with the Samaritan woman (John 4), it is clear that as saints function together *place is a non-issue*. It's not about the "correct" mountain, store-front or home. On the other hand, the history of what is called "church" reveals an inordinate fixation on buildings set apart as "places of worship." Howard Snyder in 1975 illustrated from many angles the huge concerns religious properties create in his book, *The Problem of Wineskins: Church Structure in a Technological Age.* Under the New Covenant, the need for religious places has been abolished. As Christ builds His *ekklesia*, it is natural for them to gather as family in homes. They are free to gather *anywhere*, but they must be vigilant in not allowing where they meet to be a distraction, to detract from family life, or to be a financial drain. Traditional church buildings are not neutral. Their origin is suspicious at best; they are not conducive to authentic *ekklesia*; they create numerous concerns and bring no cures. Remember, *the loss of family atmosphere in the second century onwards, combined with the shift to religious structures brought about the demise of Spirit-led ekklesia.*

CHAPTER 4
Family Is Hospitality

Hebrews 3 tells us that the Old Covenant house of Moses was superseded by the New Covenant "house" of Christ. We are the *home* where He dwells. A home should be a place where *hospitality* is extended to others. Those with larger dwellings in the first century opened their homes as a setting where the saints could both feast and eat and drink of Christ together.

Have you ever considered the gathering of Jesus-followers as fundamentally a setting where Jesus opens His home to us? Have you thought about our gathering together as a manifestation of His hospitality to us? Jesus extends hospitality to us by giving us a free space, an open space in which He flows through each part by the Spirit.

Henri Nouwen saw hospitality as a paradigm through which to view all of our relationships—husband/wife, parents/children, teachers/students and healers/patients. Hospitality, he said is "primarily the creation of a free space where the stranger can enter and become a friend instead of an enemy. Hospitality is not to change people, but to offer them space where change can take place…we can offer a space where people are encouraged to disarm themselves, to lay aside their occupations and preoccupations…Just as we cannot force a plant to grow, but can take away the weeds and stones which prevent its development, so we cannot force anyone to such a personal and intimate change of heart, but we can offer the space where such a change can take place."

Nouwen suggested that we all desperately need the hospitality of free space in order to grow in Christ: "if we expect any salvation, redemption, healing and new life, *the first thing we need is an open receptive place where something can happen to us...*" But immediately several serious problems arise in our minds. Right away we might jump to these thoughts: *Where can I find such a loving, open group? Do such groups even exist?* Sadly, the structures of most churches do not allow hospitable open space. "Basically," Clyde Reid observed in 1966, "we do not want anything to happen on Sunday morning that will upset our daily routine. We want to be 'inspired,' to come away with a warm feeling, but we do not want to be disturbed. So subconsciously we structure the service in order to assure safe, predictable, comfortable results."

Then, this very troubling question probably appears, *Even if I found myself in such a hospitable, receptive setting, am I open, ready and prepared to participate in it?*

Nouwen knew that hospitable space is "far from easy in our occupied and preoccupied society." He stepped on our toes when he rightly pointed out our propensity to avoid both silence and challenge:

> "From a distance, it appears that we try to keep each other filled with words and actions, without tolerance for a moment of silence...We are so afraid of open spaces and empty places that we occupy them with our minds even before we are there... We indeed have become a very preoccupied people, afraid of unnamable emptiness and silent solitude.
>
> In fact, our preoccupations prevent our having new experiences and keep us hanging on to the familiar ways. Preoccupations are our fearful ways of keeping things the same, and it often seems that we prefer a bad certainty to a good uncertainty. Our preoccupations help us to maintain the personal world we have created over the years, and block the way to revolutionary change. Our fears, uncertainties and hostilities make us fill

our inner world with ideas, opinions, judgments and values to which we cling as to a precious property.

Instead of facing the challenge of new worlds opening themselves for us, and struggling in the open field, we hide behind the walls of our concerns, holding on to the familiar life items we have collected in the past..." (*Reaching Out*, pp. 51-54).

Christ offers us open hospitality when we gather as His house. The atmosphere He engenders is accepting, non-condemning, non-judgmental, caring and compassionate. The issue is, *Are we passionate about participating in and contributing to such an open, receptive setting with other believers where we live?*

Can you begin to see the importance of viewing our life together in Christ through the lens of hospitality? *He graciously extends hospitality of free space to us, and we in turn extend open hospitality to one another.* It is in this climate that we can be honest, vulnerable and discover true growth as persons.

CHAPTER 5

Family Is Ekklesia

Please put on your thinking caps for reading this section. It is hard to know where to start. There are so many layers of issues, but at the end of the day the tragedy is that most people's assumptions about "church" are false, and the truth is buried in the cemetery behind the church building.

"Church" is the English word used in most versions of the Bible to translate the Greek word *ekklesia*. For example, Jesus said, "I will build My *ekklesia*..." Most English Bibles rendered this, "I will build My church." The truth is, "church" is a terrible translation of *ekklesia*.

You can Google "church or ekklesia?" and find out why "church" is manifestly inappropriate. But here is a concrete illustration of a serious problem. When Tyndale's English translation of the New Testament appeared in 1526, he correctly rendered *ekklesia* as "congregation" or "assembly." But on two occasions, Acts 14:13 and 19:37, he translated *ekklesia* as *churche* because it referred to pagan places of worship. Isn't that fascinating?

Out of the 115 times *ekklesia* occurs in the NT, the King James Version rendered it "church" 112 times. Three times, Acts 19:32, 39, 41, it translated it as "congregation," because a non-Christian gathering was in view. Isn't that interesting!

The word "church" should be purged from our vocabulary. It had its origins in paganism, communicates nothing authentic, masks the life of Christ in the body, and usually visually is connected to buildings that appear every half-mile in America.

Yet this is the word embedded in people's minds when they think of "Christianity."

Authenticity is to be found in what the word *ekklesia* meant in Jesus' and Paul's day. Don't forget, Jesus said He is building "My *ekklesia*," not "church." Jesus' disciples would have been familiar with this word in two ways.

First, it was used in the Greek translation of the Old Testament (called the *Septuagint*) to translate the Hebrew word *Qahal*. This referred to the Israelites *as assembled together*, often before the Lord.

Secondly, *ekklesia* was commonly used in the civil realm and had in view *a duly assembled group of citizens who came together to discuss and take care of common concerns in the community.*

Thus, this word primarily had both a spiritual and civil usage in the first century. Out of many choices, Jesus selected this word to define His building project. He used *ekklesia* three times in Matthew, once in chapter 16, and twice in chapter 18. In light of all the revealed dimensions, *ekklesia* must be defined as *the Lord's people gathered together to carry out the whole gamut of Christ's kingdom purposes.* In light of what *ekklesia* actually entails, we need to expand our horizons. We are used to thinking of "church" in terms of going to a building, sitting in pews, working our way through a bulletin, singing a few songs, hearing a sermon, shaking some hands and going home. But the NT expression of *ekklesia* involves much, much more—especially the dimension of being a problem-solving community.

Matthew 18:19 is often quoted at prayer meetings and appears on plaques in homes—"if two of you agree on earth concerning anything they ask, it will be done for them by My Father in heaven." The problem is, the crucial context is usually forgotten when this verse is cited. The setting is one where the saints are dealing with unrepentant sin. It is here that Christ used *ekklesia* twice. "And if he/she refuses to hear them, ▮ to the *ekklesia*. But if he/she refuses even to hear the *ekklesia*, let him/her be to you like a heathen and a tax collector."

Matthew 18:15-20 shows that the saints comprise a problem-solving community. Notice that the *body* handles the issue. There is nothing in the passage about "the leaders" doing anything. The concern is brought to the *ekklesia*.

Paul's letter to the Corinthians also shows that the *ekklesia* is called upon to deal with a wide spectrum of thorny issues.

- The saints clustered around personalities; they were to repair the breach and be one-minded

- There was serious immorality going on; they were to gather together and take care of the problem

- There were disputes being taken to unbelieving judges; they were to resolve such matters among themselves

- There were inconsiderate, divisive actions taking place in their eating together; they were to wait for one another

- There were disruptions going on in their gathering; they were to let everything be done for the building up of one another

More could be listed, but you can see how Paul assumed that the saints could take care of difficult problems by the Spirit's help, instead of defaulting to specific leaders. Again, notice that Paul never directed any remarks specifically to "leaders." *He addressed the letter to the brothers and sisters.*

This is why I try to use the word "church" for what goes on in the religious world, and the word *congregation or assembly* for authentic *ekklesia*. You can see pretty obviously that the matters the early assemblies tackled are almost never touched you ever heard of a local church helping

ımong its members—with or without the

lers"?

ent when a body of Christ-followers is

ı and to one another to pursue all aspects
of His kingdom, as we have pointed out in Matthew 18 and 1
Corinthians. You can do "church" without *ekklesia* being present.
"Church" can be carried out without commitment to anything
beyond going to a building, singing some songs, putting some
money in the plate, and listening to a sermon.

In light of what we've seen is entailed in *ekklesia*, a serious
misconception needs to be corrected. I don't know how many
times I've heard preachers/Bible teachers say, "*Ekklesia* means
the people who are 'called out.'" I hope you can see that putting
it like this totally takes the edge off of the word, and makes it
innocuous. *Ekklesia* involves spiritual commitment with others
to pursue the will of Christ. "Church" is something which, as
R.C. Sproul confessed, you go to primarily to hear a sermon.

"Binding and loosing" was a function in the Jewish culture
that only the Rabbis carried out. People would come to them
with ethical dilemmas, and they would forbid ("bind") or
allow ("loose") based on their understanding of the Law and
the traditions of the elders. However, in Matthew 18:18 Christ
grants this "binding/loosing" function to the *ekklesia* as they
take care of kingdom business. That which was limited to the
"clergy" of the Jewish religion, Jesus conferred on all His people
as they gathered. This highlights again how the body of Christ is
a Spirit-led, decision-making organism.

Our study of *ekklesia* also uncovers the fallacy of the idea that
"church" consists of meeting with people for coffee occasion-
ally. The functioning of *ekklesia* revealed in the NT involves a
group of believers in a locale. For many believers in our culture

right now, meeting from time to time with others for fellowship is all they have, but the NT concept of *ekklesia* is more robust than that. Paul could write a letter to an identifiable group of saints in a city. How could a problem be "taken to the *ekklesia*" if there is no group of believers committed to their Lord and each other? How could disputes be resolved by a few people who meet for coffee periodically? The NT assumed that believers were in ongoing relationships where the 58 "one anothers" would be meaningful ("comfort one another," "prefer one another," etc.).

Because the word "church" has so much incorrect baggage and human tradition attached to it, most people have become desensitized to the actual realities of our identity as Christ's *ekklesia*. We would do well, then, to consider this crisp summary of the word:

> "We belong to a heavenly political system called the *Kingdom of God*, and we have a King called Jesus the Christ. We all are heavenly citizens of the '*ekklesia* of God' and we come together purposely to make Spirit-led judicial *policies* and *decisions* in light of the Kingdom of God on earth, that is, we participate in binding and loosing" (Skeeter Wilson, 2001, author of *Crossing Rivers*).

In light of what is really wrapped up in who we are as the *ekklesia*, all vestiges of "church" should be jettisoned. *Ekklesia* is the life of Christ flowing through the saints to carry out His purposes. There's a whole lot of "church" going on, but how much *ekklesia life* is really occurring?

CHAPTER 6
Family Is Freedom

There are continual refrains one hears from believers who have moved from "church" to *ekklesia*. They go something like this: "I began to know that Christ had important contributions for me to share with the others; I realized that an open atmosphere where everyone can share is healthy, and promotes our growth in Christ; through honest relationships, I began to experience healing in my own life."

Why is it that people often blossom when they leave an institution and begin to function in an atmosphere where Christ's life is welcome? Because they experience *freedom* in a setting of loving hospitality—where Jesus is giving them space in His home, and they then extend space to others.

In order to highlight the contrast between institutional closed space and open space with family, I will use Shaun McNiff's narrative, found in his book *Art Heals*, concerning the art therapy he began in 1970. As you read this narrative, connect "family" with the art studio, and connect "institution" with the hospital. Shaun gathered residents in mental institutions and had them come into "a physical space that called for their involvement." The 1960's-1970's were a time "when patients were institutionalized and there were few treatment opportunities other than psychiatric drugs and the use of restraints, but considerable space was being made available for art."

Institutional Atmosphere Stifling

"My supervisor was a psychiatrist who felt that the most important therapeutic work occurred within groups and communities. He was deeply suspicious of the medical model in mental health, and we didn't have to look far in the hospital to see its failures manifested by the 'bureaupathic' ways people treated each other."

"We had to get out of the hospital to establish a sanctuary of soul medicine that functioned according to a totally different vision of treatment. Within the hospital, institutional forces swallowed every attempt at change."

"Today," Jean Vanier remarked, "hospitals and asylums may be cleaner, but the same men and women are still there crying out for a home and for love. *Big institutions cannot be a home.*"

The Studio Was "Another World"

"It was an asylum within the asylum because of its separation from the main hospital complex. Patients entering the studio environment literally passed into another world, possessed of distinctly different qualities than what they encountered on the wards."

Hospitality that Fostered Healing and Personal Growth

"We establish a community of creation through the basic actions of working together and reflecting on one another's expressions."

"We discovered that empowering the patient artists as decision-makers and creators increased their sense of belonging and responsibility. [Maxwell] Jones felt that the creative transformation was stimulated by a 'social ecology' involving flexible and open interaction, listening, the sharing of decisions, learning from mistakes, trust in people, and a pervasive sense that process was more important than the goal itself."

"A totally free space free of judgment, enabled them to explore challenging areas for the first time…Creative powers are exercised when people feel safe."

The Group Synergy is Greater than Any One Part

"We relax our self-consciousness and become part of a larger group expression."

"The group mind is more intelligent, creative, and resourceful than any one of us...What we need to express will naturally emanate from our interactions if we can stay open, committed, and patient, affirm each other; let go; and trust the process."

"Groups are capable of generating much more energy and power than a person acting alone."

What Happens in Open Space Is Unpredictable

"The journey will take us to surprising and unexpected places if we submit to it, and the most significant discoveries cannot be planned in advance."

"The distinct features of the process cannot be predicted: this is what most thoroughly distinguishes the healing qualities of the studio from medical science."

"So much of therapeutic culture has been concerned with the technical fixing of problems; yet the real work of art and healing may have more to do with what the Romantic poets called flying sparks, which jump from person, image to person, person to image, and image to image in unpredictable ways."

Simple Hospitality Goes Deep

"Depth and simplicity are bound together. 'The simpler the deeper,' I like to say."

WHAT HAPPENS WHEN PEOPLE EXPERIENCE HOSPITABLE OPEN SPACE?

Shaun talks about his early years, 1970-1974, in connection with three patients, Anthony, Bernice and Christopher. They each illustrate in different ways how expressing themselves in an open space contributed to their blossoming as human beings.

Anthony

Anthony was institutionalized at age 15. Shaun met him when he was 34, and worked with him on and off for eight years. Anthony had no "extended eye contact with people or things for so many years."

In some open space in "the back ward of an aging mental hospital," Shaun encouraged Anthony, and he finally made some simple drawings. As Anthony progressed, Shaun was amazed at his attention to detail and his shift from monochromatic to vivid colors in his art work.

Then as Anthony began to have eye contact with the world around him through artistic expression in open space, a *relational* dimension emerged. "After being totally nonverbal for so many years, Anthony began to speak with other people. The first time he spoke spontaneously to me, he leaned his face toward mine and said, 'I can talk to you'...A few minutes later he said, 'I've been dead for a long time, but I'm alive now.'"

His "artistic accomplishments stimulated corresponding changes in Anthony's overall behavior. He began working regularly in the hospital laundry and moved out of the locked ward and into a therapeutic community program for men and women."

Bernice

Shaun worked with Bernice for three months. She had "withdrawn from all contact with people and sat in a motionless state on the hospital ward." Doing art in open space allowed her to let out anger and sadness that she had previously held inside. "As her art developed she started to talk to me and to others."

Then, as she "began to speak, she simultaneously started to use vivid colors in her pictures." In her case, as she got better and better socially, her interest in art receded.

Christopher

Christopher was 58 when he came into the art studio. He had been in the state hospital for 35 years. His beginnings as an artist were self-initiated, and after a while he moved from copying the work of others to doing his own renditions. His growing artistic abilities "revealed a definite intelligence that had gone unrecognized for many years of institutional life." His artistic competence was especially amazing in light of only a "minimal elementary-school level of education and many years of isolation within state institutions."

Christopher's development as an artist was "paralleled by enhanced skills in relating to people." He also began to "talk regularly about leaving the hospital and living on his own... Christopher ultimately left Danvers after more than thirty-five years, to live with his family in a nearby community." His art was exhibited at the School of the Museum of Fine Arts in Boston. His exhibit was "well received by art critics in all of the Boston newspapers, and the *Globe* critic selected it as one of the city's finest exhibitions for the year 1974."

It is a sociological axiom that those who come out of restrictive, stifling and closed institutions very often thrive when they come into *a family atmosphere*, where there is love, acceptance, openness and genuine caring. Shaun saw over and over that "individualistic self-expression needed a place where it could be cultivated, witnessed, and affirmed by others. The healing and life-enhancing powers of art are closely tied to relationships with other people."

"Art heals," Shaun notes, "by transforming isolation and connecting us to others, to place and to ourselves in life-affirming ways. We support the creativity of others and their healing through art by *establishing environments where this interplay can take place.*"

Jean Vanier worked with challenged persons in community for over thirty years. "My experience has shown," he recounted, "that when we welcome people from this world of anguish, brokenness and depression, when they gradually discover that they are wanted and loved as they are and that they have a place, then we witness a real transformation—I would even say 'resurrection'...As they discover a sense of belonging, that they are part of a 'family,' then the will to live begins to emerge."

The hospitable atmosphere of a family, similar to Shaun's art studios, is the foundation of healthy *ekklesia*. We need a Bethany, as Frank Viola pointed out in *God's Favorite Place on Earth*, a family *where Jesus is welcome*, in every city and village!

CHAPTER 7
Family Is Safe

It is difficult to write about safe-ness in a family because there are so many variables and chemistries going on simultaneously. Further, no group will be squeaky-clean safe, and you cannot give the impression that only safe people are welcome in it. So we will explore the questions, *Am I safe as an individual?* and *Are we safe as a group?*

As we mentioned before, each person has built into them as image-bearers the desire to *be with* others. From another angle this translates into longing for a *safe place.* Because of our fallen world, a lot of us were set back personally at different points and periods in our lives because we sought to be, or were forced to be with others in very unsafe places—places where we were abused, exploited, wounded and manipulated. Is it any wonder that vast multitudes are gun-shy of relationships when their past tells them, as Henri Nouwen noted, "that there is no one who cares and offers love without conditions, and no place where we can be vulnerable without being used"? Whether they know it or not, most people are looking for a safe place. In fact, Henri Nouwen made the point that at the core of human existence is the need for a safe place. In this regard, each of us would do well to consider what Nouwen said in his talks on The Prodigal Son:

> "What I'd like you to think about is that it is very, very important to feel safe. And one of the things that I'm more and more aware of is how important it is for you, for me, for us to have a safe place. Where can you be really safe? Somehow the spiritual journey is a journey that requires that we have a deep, deep sense of safety.

We are afraid precisely because we do not really feel safe. And for me one of the most important questions is, 'Where am I safe?' With whom am I safe? Where can I let myself be known in a safe way? And there are always limitations it seems. Yes, it is safe, but there is still this or that makes it unsafe.

And I do hope that you discover more and more where it's safe for you. We have to start discovering that safety with each other, in nature, you have to discover that safety in the physical space where you are, you have to discover that safety in prayer, and you have to discover that safety with God.

And you will discover the more you reflect on your life how afraid you are. And it can sometimes be just the building that scares you, or it can be just the water that makes you afraid, or the clouds, or a certain person that scares you—not that he/she is not nice or not friendly—but you feel uncomfortable. And it comes from a place you don't even understand—why am I a little scared to talk with that person? why am I afraid I might say the wrong thing?—and you discover you are not safe there. And with God you don't feel safe. A little bit here, a little bit there, but not really feeling safe all the time.

And my deepest conviction is that once you have a place where you are safe, that's the place where you always can return. But if you don't have a safe place to return to, all of your life becomes scary, because you never know where to go back to.

And all I want to do in this series on the Prodigal Son is to give you an image of safety, a return to the place where it is safe, and probably the most useful word for that is 'womb,' the womb of God. That's the safest place. A lot of us weren't even safe in the womb because our mothers were sometimes also afraid, and somehow there is no human being who hasn't experienced very early on the fears of those around him or her. We carry that in our lives.

The spiritual life is to discover that there is safety for us. And that God wants to offer us that safe place where we can dwell, and where we can return to, and then we can let our whole body and mind and heart sort of stay without fear. And I'm really convinced that in order to be strong, to take risks, to do new things, we have to be able to be totally safe somewhere else where we can return to." (Henri Nouwen, "The Return of the Prodigal Son," 1998, Tape #2, "The Older Son" [cassette]).

As we reflect on our journeys we can probably see how we've stepped into places we thought were safe, but they weren't, and we've been part of safe settings for varying periods of time. Those safe places we've discovered over time perhaps have been different in configuration—a neighboring family, an individual, a circle of close friends, a group of believers, and, yes, even a special spot where you find yourself to be alone.

What was it in those healthy settings that made us feel safe? The key components were likely that we *felt accepted in the place we were at*, that we were *loved without conditions*, and that *we were not sitting under the judgment of others*.

So we ask ourselves, Am I a safe person? Perhaps we struggle with judging others, wanting to control and manipulate others, and being easily offended at every turn. If such tendencies in yourself concern you, then ask the Lord to work His life out in you in light of Henri Nouwen's counsel:

"When we are free from the need to judge or condemn, we can become safe places for people to meet in vulnerability, and take down the walls that separate them…When people realize that we have no hidden agendas or unspoken intentions, that we are not trying to gain any profit for ourselves, that our only desire is peace and reconciliation, they may find the inner freedom and courage to leave their guns at the door and enter into conversation with their enemies…Many times this happens even without our planning. Our service of reconciliation most often takes place when we ourselves are least aware of it. Our simple, non-judgmental presence does it."

Of course, there are always many details that each of us wrestles with, but I think Nouwen has captured in those words the *essence* of what it means to be a safe individual. People sense when you come to them with no personal agendas, versus when you are laden with self-serving baggage.

Then what is entailed in a group being safe? There is something in this that is very intuitive, that is caught more than taught. Most of you have experienced this firsthand. When you come into a group, usually within minutes you can tell if you are freely accepted or if there are hoops you must jump through to be "in." It just does not take long for you to know whether you are safe in a group. Now sometimes your initial reactions may turn out to be mistaken because of your own issues, but usually your first vibes are pretty much on target.

What elements are present when we feel unsafe? We feel like outsiders until we are initiated into whatever their key doctrine or experience may be. Put another way, we feel left out until we jump through the hoops the group has erected as grounds for acceptance. Graphic example: in the group, the King James Version only is used, and you come in with the New Revised Standard Version. Another component of feeling unsafe would be that you feel judged, out of place, because of your color, gender, economic status, educational level, or general background. We feel second class because we do not fit the group's profile of what is acceptable.

A safe family will be cultivating a *welcoming*, accepting atmosphere where the heart throb is *Jesus Christ plus nothing*. A Gospel community sees itself as accepted in the Beloved, so it has nothing to prove, and nothing to impose on others. A Jesus-family knows that its salvation is rooted in His performance, not theirs, and thus it can extend grace and kindness to others in a loving, non-judgmental atmosphere. Christ's family knows that their sins—that pile up to heaven—have been forgiven, and thus they have no basis to choke others over a dime that is owed to them. Believers who are safe and secure in Christ make up a safe family where growth can occur.

At this point, a reminder is appropriate. In the Old Testament there were certain *Cities of Refuge* where under dire circumstances people could find an assured place of safety until justice could be carried out. Of course, Jesus is our *City of Refuge* par excellence. But He desires for there to be Bethanys on earth, places where Jesus is welcome and where the needy can come (perhaps, *run*) for safety and love. Are we ready to be this kind of *City?*

Charles Foster, *The Story of the Bible*, 1884

I must add that having a loving, safe community does not mean there is never correction. In Romans 15, Paul brought out two vital and connected dimensions of body-life. In verse 7, we are to *accept one another* in Christ. In verse 15, he mentioned that the saints were also "able to *admonish each other.*" The

divine order is that care and correction flow out of acceptance.
If you have a loving setting with no concern for one another,
you will end up with a mere social club. If you have attempted
correction without full acceptance, you will end up with a witch
hunt. What the Lord has put together, we must not separate.
Correction must come as an extension of deepening relationships in a safe family.

CHAPTER 8
Family Is...Imperfect

As we have talked about ideals in Jesus' family, we must face the reality that *ekklesia* in this age is far from perfect. After people commit to following Christ, "then Jesus calls his friends into community with others who have been chosen for the same path." Jean Vanier went on to say, "This is when all the problems begin! We see the disciples squabbling among themselves, wondering who is the greatest, the most important among them! Community is a wonderful place, it is life-giving; but it is also a place of pain because it is a place of truth and of growth—the revelation of our pride, our fear, and our brokenness."

Years ago Vernon Grounds wrote a terrific article, "Fellowship of Porcupines," in which he pointed out that we all are capable of poking each other with our quills. Most of the time we don't mean to, but it happens nevertheless. That is why Paul knew Christ's family had to be a *community of forgiveness*. "Bear with each other and forgive one another; if any of you has a grievance against someone, forgive as the Lord forgave you." Paul knew there would be rough spots in the Body, but he encouraged the saints to let the Lord's life flow through them in kindness, just as they had received from Him.

The truth is, many of us struggle with imperfection in the Lord's family. A lot of the time this occurs because we are longing for that *safe family*, and often it seems to take years to find it. After we function with joy in it for a season, we soon learn that it's not the utopia we thought it would be. Then we then sink into various negative reactions.

Henri Nouwen spoke about the dangers of desperate people looking for a "final solution." "It is sad to see," Nouwen said,

"how people suffering from loneliness, often deepened by the lack of affection in their intimate family circle, search for a final solution for their pains and look at a new friend, a new lover or a new community with Messianic expectations. Although their mind knows about their self-deceit, their hearts keep saying, 'Maybe this time I have found what I have knowingly or unknowingly been searching for.' It is indeed amazing at first sight that men and women who have had such distressing relationships with their parents, brothers or sisters can throw themselves blindly into relationships with far-reaching consequences in the hope that from now on things will be totally different."

When we come into a spiritual family with the highest of expectations, thinking *this is it*, we run the risk of creating even deeper problems. Nouwen underscored the point, "by burdening others with these divine expectations, of which we ourselves are often only partially aware, we might inhibit the expression of free friendship and love, and evoke instead feelings of inadequacy and weakness. Friendship and love cannot develop when there is an anxious clinging to each other."

We simply must have a realistic, not utopian view of *ekklesia*. Unconsciously looking for "the perfect community" will always end in disaster. Again, Nouwen astutely observed, "To wait for moments or places where no pain exists, no separation is felt, and where all human restlessness has turned into inner peace is waiting for a dreamworld. No friend or lover, no husband or wife, no community or commune will be able to put to rest our deepest cravings for unity and wholeness."

We see Christ in each other, we don't look at one another after the flesh, but we also can't forget that we are capable of letting each other down. Jean Vanier aptly captured this needed balance:

"Communion means accepting people just as they are, with all their limits and inner pain, but also with their gifts and their beauty and their capacity to grow—to see the beauty inside all the pain."

CHAPTER 9
Family Meats Together

In the first century, the Greek word for meat (*broma*) could refer to a steak, to food in general, or to that which satisfies one's longings, such as when Jesus declared, "My meat is to do the will of Him who sent me." The New Testament narrative is clear that the saints ate together ("broke bread") quite often.

It is probably safe to say that generally we have lost the "specialness" of our meals with others. I hope that what is presented in this chapter will awaken you to a deeper sensitivity to this dimension of our life together in Christ. The Lord has made us so that we need to eat, but there are beautiful aspects of eating connected to Jesus that perhaps have fallen by the wayside.

In Exodus 24 a very sobering scene unfolded after the Law-covenant was ratified by the sprinkling of blood on the altar and the people. "Moses said, 'This is the blood of the covenant which the Lord has made with you according to all these words.' Then Moses went up with Aaron, Nadab, Abihu and the 70 elders of Israel, and they saw the God of Israel. Under His feet there was a paved work of sapphire stone, as bright blue as the sky. But God did not raise His hand against these leaders of the Israelites; *they saw God, and they ate and drank.*" Given the blazing intensity of what happened here, one might think that eating and drinking would hardly be appropriate. But it was. *They saw God and had a meal.*

All of this pointed to a meal that would take place over a thousand years later on the night of Jesus' betrayal. "Then He took the cup, and gave thanks, and gave it to them, saying, 'For this is the blood of the new covenant, which is shed for many for the remission of sins.'" We are compelled to say, *they saw the Lord while eating and drinking at a meal.* And that night a *better* and a *new* covenant was inaugurated—one written on human hearts, not on tablets of stone.

We eat now in this age in remembrance of our Lord, but we also look for a glorious banquet in the age to come. Isaiah painted this prophetic picture of something far better than any buffet we could enjoy these days:

> "On this mountain the Lord Almighty will prepare a feast of rich food for all peoples, a banquet of aged wine—the best of meats and the finest of wines. On this mountain he will destroy the shroud that enfolds all peoples, the sheet that covers all nations; he will swallow up death forever. The Sovereign Lord will wipe away the tears from all faces; he will remove his people's disgrace from all the earth."

Now here's the mind-blowing part of this wedding feast. Picture the Bride of Christ sitting around a humongous table at the wedding feast of the Lamb. They are all waiting for the banquet to be served. The kitchen door swings open and out comes Jesus, bringing His Beloved a lavish meal. "He will dress Himself to serve, will have them recline at the table, and will come and wait on them" (Luke 12:37). The Lord Himself will be our Waiter!

> "Then I heard what seemed to be the voice of a great multitude, like the roar of many waters and like the sound of mighty peals of thunder, crying out,
>
> 'Hallelujah!
> For the Lord our God
>   the Almighty reigns.
> Let us rejoice and exult
>   and give him the glory,
> for the marriage of the Lamb has come,
>   and his Bride has made herself ready;
> it was granted her to clothe herself
>   with fine linen, bright and pure'—

for the fine linen is the righteous deeds of the saints. And the angel said to me, 'Write this: Blessed are those who are invited to the marriage supper of the Lamb.' And he said to me, 'These are the true words of God.'"

So all of history ultimately is about Father obtaining a Bride for His Son, and the Lamb and His wife consummating in a wedding meal in the New Heaven and New Earth. These realities should shape our thoughts as we enjoy meals together now on earth.

In Acts 20:6-7 we are given a little glimpse of first century ekklesia-life.

"But we sailed away from Philippi after the Days of Unleavened Bread, and in five days joined them at Troas, where we stayed seven days. Now on the first day after the Sabbath, when *the disciples assembled together to break bread*, Paul, ready to depart the next day, dialogued with them and continued his talk until midnight."

Why do believers gather? In Acts 20:7 the infinitive of purpose ("to break") clearly reveals that *they gathered for the purpose of breaking bread*—in other words, to feast on Jesus as they ate together. The stated *reason* for the meeting was not to sing, or hear a "sermon," but to remember the Lord in a love feast (*agape*). Howard Marshall pointed out that in the earliest *ekklesias* "a meal accompanied the Lord's Supper at this time," and J.B. Lightfoot noted that "the heart of the festival" was the breaking of bread (Marshall, *The Acts of the Apostles*, Eerdmans, 1983, p. 327; Lightfoot, *The Acts of the Apostles: A Newly Discovered Commentary*, IVP, 2014, p. 261). It is safe to say that most entities called churches do not gather in order to break bread. It would seem in most cases, as R.C. Sproul mentioned, "in Protestant worship, for the most part, *we sit and listen to a sermon.*" When our identity as *family* is lost, the breaking of bread is rendered superfluous.

We have seen in snapshots throughout the biblical narrative how *the Lord meets us in our corporate meals.* Three perspectives dominate as we enjoy our *ekklesia* food. Jesus directed us to *look back* and remember His sacrificial death for us. We are *now* to consider that the one loaf and one cup reveal to us that we are one body and members one of another. And we *look forward* to the glorious marriage supper of the Lamb and His Bride.

Charlotte Stevens, Florida

How does all this work out in *ekklesias?* All of us have probably felt awkward at occasions where the "Lord's Supper" was done in various ways. In light of what I've shared, maybe we can sort through this a bit. First of all, we need to come to terms with the fact that the Lord attaches deep meaning to our eating together. He knows it is all about Himself, and desires for us to thank and praise Him. Next, we need to ask the Lord by His Spirit to make us very sensitive to the reality that our Body meals are occasions to express Jesus to each other. There are two mistakes to be avoided. One would be the pressure to make sure Jesus' name is mentioned every time saints eat together. The other would be to trivialize our meals by never reminding one another of the past, present and future dimensions of our eating and drinking. The only way for these concerns to be avoided is if the saints are sensitized by the Spirit to the truth that *our earthly meals point in all directions to Jesus Christ, and ultimately to His long-awaited wedding supper with His Bride.* Thus, we should not want our remembrance of Him to be a religious ritual we go through, and we should not want our food-fellowship to be void of the fullness of the Son of God. The Spirit will direct us as we walk this fine line.

In the early *ekklesias* the brothers and sisters ate a meal together and remembered the Lord in various ways. In time, however, the "Eucharist" was separated from the meal. Later, then, the meal was eliminated and "the bishop" had to "administer" the Eucharist. The *family meal* was gone and the *institutional "sacrament"* took its place. Emil Brunner astutely pointed out that the changes that took place regarding the Lord's Supper provided "the starting point for the later institutional development, the movement by which the early Christian community became a Church" (*Misunderstanding*, p. 66). What was at first a simple meal around the Lord became a "sacrament" under the thumb of church leaders. The word "sacrament" is unacceptable to use in the context of *ekklesia* life in Christ. Again, Brunner called attention to the fact that "New Testament Christianity knows nothing of the word 'sacrament,' which belongs essentially to the heathen world of the Graeco-Roman empire, and which unfortunately some of the Reformers unthinkingly took over from ecclesiastical tradition. For this word, and still more the overtones which it conveys, is the starting point for those disastrous developments which began soon to transform the community of Jesus into the Church, which is first and foremost a sacramental Church" (*Misunderstanding*, pp. 72-73). Tragically, what first began as a *family full of life, freedom and breaking bread with gladness* was transformed into an *institution full of church leaders in control, especially of the "sacraments."*

CHAPTER 10
Family Meets Together

Many families get in the car on Sunday morning and head to a building in order to attend a "worship service." Most often an usher will hand a bulletin to those entering that tells the order of what will happen—when to sing, when to stand and sit, when to put money in the plate, when to listen to the pastor's sermon, and when to leave after the benediction.

Is there any evidence that the early church had a "worship service" similar to what is printed in church bulletins? Absolutely none. Just as there is revelation in 1 Corinthians 11 about the saints eating together as family, so there is revelation in 1 Corinthians 14 about the brethren coming together as an *ekklesia*. The question that begs for an answer is, *Why have we constructed a "service" that focuses on one person's monologue, and totally ignores the open meeting Paul encouraged in which "each one of you has a contribution; let all things be done for building up one another."*

William Barclay, who was a member in the very liturgical Church of Scotland, said this about the Body gathering described in 1 Cor. 14—"It sheds a flood of light on what a church service was like in the early Church. There was obviously a freedom and informality about it, which is completely strange to our ideas… There was clearly no settled order at all…The really notable thing about an early church service must have been that almost everyone came feeling that they had both the privilege and the obligation of contributing something to it."

"Now Paul sketches [in 1 Cor. 14] a picture of worship, a very flexible procedure," William A. Beardslee commented, which is "to be open to anyone, but each is to be attentive to the good of all…What a revealing glimpse of a vital community, whose worship was in good measure unstructured, open to participation by all, and guided not by a pre-set program, but by the Spirit!…Apparently there was no one who regularly presided, in contrast to the almost universal practice of the later church" (*First Corinthians: A Commentary for Today*, Chalice Press, 1994, pp. 136-137).

Ernest F. Scott in 1941 highlighted the chasm between the synagogue and early gatherings of believers, and how its simplicity moved more and more to complexity as time elapsed.

"[The ekklesia] was not the Jewish community over again, with a few minor differences, but was a new creation…[W]hen much of his spiritual teaching was forgotten…the church took on more and more of the character of an ordinary society. It sought its models deliberately in the guilds and corporations of the day, and before a century had passed a Christian church was almost a replica in miniature of a Roman municipality. It had a body of officers graded like those of the city, clothed in similar vestments and bearing similar titles. The conception of a unique society, representing on earth the new order which would prevail in the Kingdom, seemed almost to have disappeared" *(The Nature of the Early Church*, Charles Scribner's Sons, 1941, pp. 31, 110).

Way back in 1898 David Thomas uncovered insight about the gathering in 1 Cor. 14:

"Is the Christian church justified in confining its attention to the *ministry of one person*? In most modern congregations there are some Christian people who by natural ability, by experimental knowledge and inspiration, are far more qualified to instruct and confront the people than their professional and stated minister. Surely official preaching has no authority, either in Scripture, reason, or experience, and it must come to an end sooner or later" (*The Pulpit Commentary: 1 Corinthians*, F.W. Farrar & David Thomas, Funk & Wagnalls, 1898, pp. 429-433).

It must be underscored that New Testament scholars and Church historians of all stripes—Catholic, Lutheran, Presbyterian, Methodist, Charismatic, secular, etc.—are in *unison* that the earliest gatherings functioned as depicted in the four quotations above, and later morphed into a period that was led by a leader. The participation of all was displaced by a service that rendered the attendees as passive onlookers to what was going on up-front.

In the early church gatherings, every family member could express their portion of the infinite Christ as the Spirit led. What a blessing to hear the Living Christ as He flowed out of those in whom He lived! *Expression*. That's what a body is for, as Frank Viola explains:

> "What is the purpose of a body? The answer: to express the life that's within it. My body gives my personality expression. In the same way, the physical body of Jesus was the instrument, or the tool, for God to manifest His personality in the earth.
>
> What had taken place [on the Day of Pentecost]? The body of Christ was born on the earth. But what does that mean? It means this: The literal body of Jesus Christ had returned to earth. And it expanded. God now had a family.
>
> Jesus Christ in heaven had dispensed Himself into His body on earth. He returned to earth in the form of His body, the church, and His species was reintroduced to the planet.
>
> Jesus Christ is now in the Spirit. And He craves expression also. He seeks to make His life visible through a many-membered being. In the eyes of God, the Church is nothing more and nothing less than Jesus Christ on earth. It's a new species that's kin to divinity; a body to the Son and a family to the Father. Kind of His own kind."

Meeting in openness and spontaneity to express the Son accords well with a *family get-together*, but not with an *institution preserving its boundaries and control.* As tragic as it is to admit this, it cannot be denied that most "worship services" impede the expression of Christ, for the structure carries on as if the body is *one part,* not many. How can the Lord be expressed through a plural body if only *one* member speaks? How can a body be healthy if the functioning falls mainly on one part? That can only be a recipe for sickness and death.

We must ask ourselves, are we being honest with the Lord's revelation? No one can deny that the *agape* meal and multi-participant meetings are present in the NT. The crucial issue is, *did they cease for valid reasons?* As he sought to justify the Roman Catholic agenda, D.I. Lanslots freely admitted:

> "The public worship or the Liturgy, which is a certain devel-opment of prayers and ceremonies, as we have it to-day, *did not exist in the days of the Apostles*…Two early ceremonies, that accompanied the celebration ['Holy Eucharist'], soon disap-peared; *they were not essential.* The first was the love-feast; the other the spiritual exercises, in which people were moved by the Holy Spirit to prophesy, speak in divers tongues, heal the sick by prayer, and so on; St. Paul in his first epistle to the Corinthians refers to these (14:1-14)" (*The Primitive Church: The Church in the Days of the Apostles* (1926), Tan Books, 1980, pp.264-265).

He freely acknowledges that the early church was marked by eating together and Spirit-led functioning as a body. But these "soon disappeared," and were replaced by a formal liturgy that was leader-dependent. Lanslots' justification for this monumen-tal shift echoes what many think or say, *"they were not essential."* Not essential? Who makes that judgment call? When these two marks of the *ekklesia* were in full force, the glory of the Lord came in power; when they were phased out, the glory of the Lord departed (Hebrew, *Ichabod*), and a lifeless institution was left standing. In light of what happened in history, are we really prepared to argue that what is found in the New Testament is "not essential"? Has it ever occurred to anyone that perhaps the reason for our sickly state is that we've abandoned the shared life of Christ that the brothers and sisters lived by in the early days?

CHAPTER 11
Family Celebrates Together

Over time every family experiences a *total* spectrum together that encompasses all the ups-and-downs life will bring. *Celebration* should be a regular part of body-life. Henri Nouwen captured a vital dimension of our shared life in Christ: "a joyful togetherness of spontaneous people." *Thankfulness* and *rejoicing* are two oft-repeated exhortations to the brothers and sisters. "Rejoice," Paul said, "and again I say, Rejoice."

A word flowing naturally out of celebration is *"remember."* On a host of occasions Israel was instructed to "remember" the many wonderful things the Lord had done for them by various concrete expressions, such as making a pile of rocks. After the Lord gave Israel victory over the Philistines on one occasion, "Samuel took a stone and set it up between Mizpah and Shen, and called it 'Ebenezer,' saying 'Thus far the Lord has helped us'" (1 Samuel 7:12). Celebrating and remembering the great deliverance the Lord accomplished in bringing Israel out of Egyptian bondage in the Red Sea exodus was woven into the fabric of their life together.

Likewise, the Lord's people now celebrate the New Exodus Christ accomplished in Jerusalem (Luke 9:31), purchasing His *ekklesia* on the cross. Our Lord told us that as often as we eat together we are to *remember* His past work in history, His present indwelling of the Body, and His future coming to bring a New Heaven and New Earth.

All the treasures of wisdom, beauty and knowledge are to be found in Christ, so there is no end to our celebration of

Him! But we can also celebrate Christ in each other and in His creation in untold ways.

I recall a road trip we did in 1984, when we visited a group in Pennsylvania. It just so happened that a good part of the meeting we were part of was devoted to recognizing and honoring the service of a brother to the Body and to the community. For several years he had spent sacrificial time helping many by repairing their vehicles, doing yard work and landscaping, refurbishing rooms in homes, painting houses, and doing plumbing work. In all his pursuits he had a humble servant spirit, and just desired to do good to all, especially to the Lord's people. When the saints honored this brother's work among them, not a few openly wept as they told of how his gifts had blessed them in their moments of need. This was a truly amazing celebration where hands were lifted in praise to the Savior's work in one of the members.

Jean Vanier brings insight to the importance of celebration after years of experience in community:

> "We must learn to celebrate. I say *learn* to celebrate because celebration is not just a spontaneous event. We have to discover what celebration is…Do we know how to celebrate our togetherness, our being one body?…We need to rediscover celebration. That is what community is all about…Celebration is to share what and who we really are; it is to express our love for one another, our hopes, and to rejoice in being called together as parts of the same body. As we go from singing, dancing and laughter into silence, there will be a sense of presence. Somewhere at the heart of celebration there is the consciousness of the presence of Christ. Christ is the one who is our cornerstone, the one who has drawn us together, and we rejoice because he is present with us…When I visit communities, I frequently ask, 'How do you celebrate?' If they say, 'We don't celebrate,' then I know the community risks death."

Over time all families and communities will go through challenges and setbacks. Some of these may threaten the very foundations of the group's life together. Spirit-led celebrations will go a long way to maintain that "joyful togetherness" that we wish to reign and flourish in our relationships in Christ's Body, while we navigate the bumps too!

CHAPTER 12
Family Is Relational

Sometimes those in the world see what is important before the church does. A secular publication rightly observed:

> "How do we become more resilient to increasing instability? Whether you're buying gold or building solar panels, your best investment is in *relationships*. It's people coming together to weather the storm that gives you your best chance at a happy, healthy life regardless of what calamities or crises you might face" (*FIC-eNews*, Dec 31, 2016).

As we noted at the beginning of this book, *reality is relational to the core*. Sin has twisted, distorted and perverted relationships, but Christ died to inaugurate a New Humanity where relationships are restored. He has purposed to build a home made of living stones, a family composed of all kinds of people who have believed in Christ. However, beginning in the Second Century something went wrong.

When everything is boiled down, the reality that Christ's family is at its core *relational* gets to the heart of the monumental tragedy that began to take root around 150AD. The early *ekklesia* saw the life of Christ coming to expression in family relationships where the 58 "one anothers" were carried out in the Spirit. The post-apostolic church lost the family atmosphere and became increasingly *institutional*. It is pivotal to understand that what was a living organism (*ekklesia*) morphed into an institutional religion (church). There was a decided shift from *focus on Christ and His Bride* to *focus on leaders and "sacraments."* There was an increasing emphasis and dependence on *structure* instead of the *Spirit*.

The conclusion of Osiek/Balch is of the utmost significance: Believers' gatherings *"no longer took place in a family environment."* When the family atmosphere disappeared, then relationships went out the door and a rigid institutionalism began to take over.

This reveals the vast chasm between *ekklesia* and *church*—in *ekklesia* loving relationships are encouraged, cultivated and can flourish; in *church* the structures generally foster settings where relationships are shallow and stifled. For sure, something is going on here that concerns pastors, for myriads of people are leaving the buildings and looking for relationships elsewhere.

Can we be shocked that churches are not fertile soil for relationships when, to a high degree, church leaders are non-relational themselves? In Bible school and seminary future pastors are taught not to get too chummy with the parishioners. Barrows Dunham noted that a person with far-reaching authority "became remote as gods are, unapproachable except by a few consecrated persons, mostly of his own family. A stifling etiquette surrounded him. He knew, in dreadful perfection, the loneliness with which power curses the powerful" (*Heroes & Heretics: A Social History of Dissent*, Alfred Knopf, 1964, p. 7).

Since the institutional system is largely non-relational, it cannot surprise us that many church leaders cannot handle close relationships. Henri Nouwen isolated a penetrating insight that should be a wake-up call for all of us:

> "One thing is clear to me: The temptation of power is greatest when intimacy is feared. Much Christian leadership is exercised by people who do not know how to develop healthy, intimate relationships and have opted for power and control instead. Many Christian empire builders have been people unable to give and receive love" (*In the Name of Jesus*, p. 79).

I think it is vital for us to be reminded that history clearly reveals that *life and relationships* are the first things to go when institutionalization sets in. Bob Lupton put it so unbelievably well in his "Cycles of Life" (September, 2010):

"Viewed against the backdrop of history, the current demise of denominations is predictable. In time, all institutions follow a similar pattern. They begin as fresh movements, new and exciting, abundant with vision and creativity. But in order to survive, a movement must develop structural strength—mission statement, doctrinal distinctives, leadership structure, decision-making processes.

Vigorous change takes place during this organizational phase as a seedling becomes established, sinking its roots and spreading its branches. Staff are hired, budgets are created, policies are instituted, goals and objectives are set, property is purchased. As the organization matures it becomes a source of security for its employees. Health insurance, vacation pay, cost of living raises, and retirement benefits are negotiated.

Gradually the mission shifts from the founding visionaries to hired employees and with each subsequent ring of management the passion that originally inspired the movement becomes slightly diluted. Marketing, management, and funding consume increasing amounts of organizational energy. With its own sturdy root system, it now commands its fair share of sunlight and space on the forest floor. By the time the organization enters the institutional phase of its development, it is fully vested in its own self-preservation.

Instead of a movement spending itself on behalf of a noble cause, it has become a respectable institution consumed with preserving its own viability and legacy. It may still use the same stirring language of its past movement days, and it may still perform important work, but it spends the lion's share of its energy on buildings, communication systems, internal politics and self-promotion to ensure its longevity. Good stewardship demands its preservation. It is the way of all institutions" (Bob

Lupton, "Cycle of Life," September, 2010, http://fcsministries.
org/urban-perspectives/page/2/).

It is a simple fact that the early church was first driven by
the life of Christ in believers, but ended up by 250 AD changing
into a leader-driven institution. James D.G. Dunn noted
that "increasing institutionalism is the clearest mark of early
Catholicism," and that "such features were absent from first
generation Christianity, though in the second generation the
picture was beginning to change" (*Unity & Diversity in the New
Testament*, Westminster Press, 1977, p. 351).

Bob Lupton suggested that "in order to survive, a movement
must develop structural strength—mission statement, doctrinal
distinctives, leadership structure, decision-making processes."
These are the crucial questions we must face: Did the original
relational life of Christ in believers have to be institutionalized
in order to survive? Was the movement from early *ekklesia*
simplicity to later church bureaucracy inevitable and good, or
a terrible distortion and tragedy? Is it necessary to move from
Spirit to Law in order to continue Christ's work?

The truth is that in our practice we have tried to
institutionalize the living Christ. That which is organic cannot
thrive in an institutional environment. The DNA does not
match. Of course, it must be said that there are people in many
church-institutions who are expressions of the living Christ. But
the living Christ is not a fit for institutional structures. It would
be like hoping that an orchid would flourish in a barren desert,
or that a cactus would do well in a rainforest. If we believe that
the simplicity of Christ is truth worth continuing, then we must
resist our tendency to move away from relationships toward
institutionalism with every fiber of our being. If believers were

satisfied with Jesus Christ alone, institutions wouldn't have a chance of taking over.

Mary Pipher perceptively noted, "Too often [health] institutions are about the needs of the institution, not of the patients" (*Another Country*, 2000, p. 167). Jesus did not come to start another religious institution with every candle and pulpit in its proper place. By giving His life in crucifixion, taking His life back in resurrection, returning to Father by His ascension, and pouring out His Spirit on the Day of Pentecost—He assured that his people would express His life in them as the Body of Christ on earth—organically and relationally, not as an institution.

It must be stressed that I am not saying that no deep relationships can occur in institutional churches. No church system can stop in-Christ relationships from coming to expression. Just like what happens when the boy-girl thing clicks, there is very little that can stop it from growing. What I am saying is that in traditional church structures deepening relationships are the rare exception, not the rule. Why? Because, as Bonnie Jaeckle pointed out, "there is limited healing in the church, because there is minimal community among God's people!"

The truth is, Jesus is uninstitutional. You shouldn't, you can't, institutionalize a Person. He said that the Spirit is like wind. You can't put wind in a box and make it happen. Inherent in wind is freedom. The only image that really captures this reality is Vine-branches, organic relationships.

I think this highlights a lot of the tensions we experience. Institutional Christianity dominates the landscape, and so well-meaning people are attempting to put Jesus in structures that do not foster the expression of His life in the saints. I believe that in the innumerable church buildings we have every 1/2 mile in America, Christ's life is still coming forth in varying degrees.

That's because even human structures and rules can't stop Him from showing up. But the disheartening tragedy is that His life appears in spite of the religious structures in which He is confined. Wouldn't it be glorious if the way believers functioned and came together welcomed and encouraged Christ to be present and expressed? Visible Christianity is trying to serve an organic Jesus in non-organic structures.

Jesus is building families where face-to-face relationships and true caring can blossom as He flows through His children.

CHAPTER 13
Family Cares for One Another

A.M. Fairbairn said in 1910 that the early church "regarded as to its internal relating, it was a family…in the apostles' day churches were so small that everyone knew every other and kept a watchful eye on one another" (*Studies in Religion & Theology— The Church: In Idea and In History*, The Macmillan Co., pp. 203, 207). The family nature of these *ekklesias* opened the door for real encouragement, support, and care to take place.

This raises a question about what we call a "family atmosphere." People intuitively know when a group has lost it. It often happens when a group grows larger and relationships thin out. There are so many levels of dynamics taking place that there is no way you can pin a number on when the family feeling will recede. It is estimated that the Corinthian body was between forty and sixty people. The point is that the earliest *ekklesias* were small enough that they could be *family* to one another. No one can argue that the larger groups that compose most American churches are in a position to function as family. Lack of a family atmosphere is one of the biggest reasons people are exiting traditional churches. They feel like a bump on a log destined to throw money in a plate, hear a sermon, and drive home to the roast in the oven.

Galatians 6:2 convincingly reveals the family-nature of the early church. "Bear one another's burdens and so fulfill the law of Christ." The false teachers were seeking to get believers back under the Law. Paul replied, "The Law is a burden no one can bear; it only brings curse because no one can fulfill it. Instead, bear the needs of others and you will fulfill the Law of Christ, which is love" (John 13:34). You simply cannot respond to the concerns of others you do not "know" in a family setting. People cannot be "known" in large groups laden with church structure.

Notice that Paul did not direct this exhortation to "the pastor" or any sub-set of "ministry leaders," but to the *entire assembly*. Burden-bearing was to be carried out by *everyone*. Also, caring for those who stumble into sin is not committed to a paid staff, but to the body, "you who are Spirit-led restore such a one in meekness" (Galatians 6:1).

In Hebrews 12:15 there is a revelation of staggering proportions that is, tragically, lost in translation. The *King James Version* renders it as, "Looking diligently lest any man fail of the grace of God; lest any root of bitterness springing up trouble you, and thereby many be defiled." *The Century Bible* has, "Be careful that no one fails to receive God's grace and begins to cause trouble among you. A person like that can ruin many of you." The *New Living Translation* does much better with " Look after each other so that none of you fails to receive the grace of God. Watch out that no poisonous root of bitterness grows up to trouble you, corrupting many." *Look after each other.* The Greek verb used here is what would be termed a *leadership* word, *episcopeo*, to oversee. We get the English word "episcopal" from it. The author, then, has applied a *leadership* verb, to oversee, to the whole body of believers.

R.C.H. Lenski makes these observations: "*Episcopos* is a bishop; the participle bids all the readers to act the part of *episcopoi*, overseers, by exercising continuous oversight of each other" (*The Interpretation of Hebrews*, p. 443). Lenski translates this verse as, "continuing to exercise oversight lest anyone be dropping away from the grace of God." Of course, such oversight is not a "ruling over," but rather a looking out and helping of each other.

Think about the implications of this statement in Hebrews. All the saints participate in the oversight, the watchful care, of the body. Historically, the verb *episcopeo* has been connected solely to "church leaders," and virtually no consideration has been given to the underlying truth that *oversight has been given to the entire ekklesia*, as we saw, for example, in Matthew 18:15-20. What business do we have to inordinately focus on "leaders," and "the pastor," when we have not begun to practice the body-care, as Lenski put it, "to act the part of *episcopoi*, overseers, by exercising continuous oversight of each other"? This highlights the sad fact that the way church is usually done buries what is important and exalts that for which there is no New Testament precedent.

Thomas Dubay felt it was best from a practical standpoint to connect *care* with love—a loving community is a *caring* community. And he indicated that one of the most foundational marks of a loving group is to be a *listening* people.

> "To care is to become one's brother, one's sister. We are interested when we are eager to listen (how many of us are *eager* to listen?) and slow to speak. Eagerness to listen to another is an especially sound index of interest because the other's statements are revelatory of his person. Perhaps the reason most of us rather speak than listen is that we are far more interested in ourselves than in others. *A caring community is a listening community*...We have already been told by the Master that without him we can do nothing at all. With him we can do it all. Which is to say that we cannot care, we cannot have community without the Lord living in the midst of the two or three gathered in His name."

To say that the *ekklesia* cares for one another, especially by attentively hearing others, raises the issue of *commitment*. Dubay said, "we conclude that a caring community is one in which the members share something of their inner lives." We know that the New Testament showed that body-life was primarily worked out by the Spirit as intertwined with 58 "one anothers". What possible sense do such imperatives as encourage one another, admonish one another, be longsuffering with each other, and be forbearing with one another make without the presence of a growing commitment to the body? The "one anothers" imply ongoing relationships in a town or region. What meaning is there in saying one should be "longsuffering" with a person they see a handful of times in a year at a coffee shop? Words like "forbearing" assume that one is rubbing shoulders with others in a committed relationship.

This reveals the huge difference between *church* and *ekklesia*. Folks can go to church and not have a stitch of loving commitment to anyone. In *ekklesia*, however, all the parts participate for the good of the whole, and for the long haul. To illustrate, ponder the deep chasm between people going to a building for a worship service, and what is seen in the meeting going on in 1 Corinthians 14. One can go to a traditional service and be committed only to come to a place and work through what is in the bulletin. But those in a 1 Cor. 14-type gathering are *participants*, and this implies a level of commitment. Those who are content with church would feel very uncomfortable in an open meeting with multiple contributions, and with no platform full of leaders. *Ekklesia* presupposes *involvement in others' lives*.

To care for others assumes a growing commitment to them. One can't care for others and be distant. "No one can help anyone," Nouwen believed, "without becoming involved, without entering with his whole person into the painful situation, without taking the risk of becoming hurt, wounded or even destroyed in the process." To be brutally honest, it would be my observation that most American church members have very little interest in "being there" to care for others. We have already noted that the church system is non-relational, so we should not be surprised that those in the pews are generally low on commitment to people.

It is striking to see the caring that immediately surfaced after the Day of Pentecost. A great host had come for the festival from many nations. Those who believed in Christ and were baptized ended up tarrying and not returning home right away. The believers in Jerusalem responded to these needs in various ways, with the amazing result that "there was not a needy person among them." Sacrificial caring marked the early *ekklesia* from the beginning.

A century later the deep caring by believers was evident in what they did during the Antonine Plague. As Rodney Stark wrote in *The Rise of Christianity*, Christians risked their lives and stayed in the afflicted cities while pagan leaders, and the general population, including physicians and nurses, fled.

CHAPTER 14
Family Is Healing

Humpty Dumpty sat on a wall,
Humpty Dumpty had a great fall;
All the king's horses and all the king's men
Couldn't put Humpty together again.

Many in our time have come to a great fall and the pharma and medical complex cannot put them back together again. What people need most is *loving support*. The *ekklesia* should provide such aid. A realistic picture of *ekklesia* is not as a castle, but as a hospital. We all come among one another as *needy*. Thus, *ekklesia* should be an environment that fosters *healing* in all its dimensions. As Hammett and Sofield remarked:

> "Every healthy group is therapeutic. Community groups should be therapeutic, inasmuch as they assist members to grow to the fullness of their life in Christ. People need to see a group of persons, motivated by the gospel and their love of God, who live in such a way that loneliness and alienation are dispelled. Unless the quality of community life improves, there will be another large exodus from the churches" (Hammett & Sofield, "Developing Healthy Christian Community," *Searching Together*, 24:3, 1996, pp.2-4).

People often think of healing in terms of the reversal of physical malady, like when Jesus lifted blindness and paralysis from afflicted persons. But we need to view healing as embracing the *whole person*. Paul said, "Be sanctified *wholly*—body, soul and spirit." All of us have areas where we need Jesus' healing to touch our lives. What place does the *ekklesia* have in helping us in such pockets of need?

It seems, though, that because of traditions, fears and lack of relationships, we have separated healing from *ekklesia*-life. Perhaps we would do well to bring our issues to the body of Christ in an appropriate way. Paul told the Corinthians to settle disputes among themselves, not before unbelieving judges. Is it possible that we often miss the blessing of bringing our needs *first* to the body for wisdom and healing before we go to doctors?[1] Didn't James say, "if any among you is sick, let them call for the mature brothers and sisters in the body to pray over them and anoint them with oil in the name of the Lord. And the prayer offered in faith will make the sick person well; the Lord will raise them up. If they have sinned, they will be forgiven. Therefore confess your sins to each other and pray for each other so that you may be healed. The prayer of a righteous person is powerful and effective." Notice that the initial reaching out for help began with the afflicted one.

I know full well that this is a complex issue, and that there are no easy answers, but please get my drift. I am saying neither that we should never go to the medical world for help, nor am I suggesting that going to doctors indicates a lack of faith, but I am suggesting that there is reason to believe that Jesus is pleased if we *first* come to Him and His Bride for wisdom and healing before we just default to the medical industry.

J. Jeffrey Means in his book, *Trauma & Evil,* pointed out three dilemmas facing the institutional churches related to the great need for emotional healing among church members. Leading up to this section he was dealing with "the profound ways evil creates and builds upon divisions within and among persons through experiences of abuse, neglect, and violence." Then he said:

The dilemmas are: (1) how to make better and more effective use of the shared life experiences of its members within the worship and life of the church, (2) how to encourage people to bring into the worship and life of the church those aspects of themselves and their life experience they are most ashamed of and split-off from, and (3) how to talk about sin in a way that takes it seriously but does not shame us or lead us to view ourselves and others dichotomously as "all good" or "all bad."

He then goes on to observe that "it is the lack of shared life experience and our propensity for keeping our lives secret from one another, especially those experiences we are most ashamed of, that is one dilemma the church must address." All of this aspect of healing rests on what has been previously brought up concerning a loving, accepting, and non-judgmental *ekklesia* atmosphere.

While the loving setting should be conducive to helping people with their shame, note that such matters must be handled in "appropriate ways." Much ministry along these lines can take place non-publicly, for example in sisters' or brothers' encounters. When breakthroughs occur it is wonderful for the body to hear of victories in Christ publicly. The key is a caring setting, based on relationships, where the saints feel safe to talk to others about areas of their life that are tearing them apart.

Traditional Christianity tends to render those in the pews as passive, and as a result most believers do not think of themselves as part of the healing processes of the *ekklesia*. Nouwen believed that the average person will "tend to underestimate their own human potentials and quickly make a referral to those who have titles." The truth is, however, that every disciple "is called upon to be a healer," and "we can never leave the task of healing to the specialist" (Nouwen). "We are all healers," Nouwen observed, "who can reach out to offer health, and we all are patients in constant need of help." It must be underscored, Nouwen said, that "we can do much more for each other than we are often aware of...A general atmosphere of careful attention by all the members of the Christian community can sometimes heal wounds before special care is demanded."

It would seem that we often forget this, but it must be remembered that the healing of persons is usually rooted in relationships. "The first and most important aspect of all healing," Nouwen noted, "is an interested effort to know the patients fully, in all their joys and pains...ups and downs...which have led them through the years to their present situation." In the healing process, "the full and real presence of people to each other" is necessary (Nouwen).

Looking at healing from the family perspective highlights how Christ in our relationships contributes to the building up of one another.

---

1. For further information along these lines, see my unpublished article, "Piggyback Pills," and Stephen Crosby's "Healing from Christ for the Nations," which is Chapter 21 in my *58 to 0—How Christ Leads Through the One Anothers*. I will email these documents to interested parties.

CHAPTER 15
Family Is Led

Family life is not connected to "leaders," but to sharing the life of Christ together. The history of the church shows that the deck is stacked toward "leaders." What Jesus began as a simple family morphed into an ecclesiastical bureaucracy dominated by powerful male leaders. This shift from Spirit-led to leader-led turned the outward church into a two-tiered religious institution—clergy and laity. Elaine Pagels documented the whole rationale for the bishop rising as supreme in post-apostolic history. She pointed out Clement of Alexandria's remark (ca. 150AD), "That whoever refuses to 'bow the neck' and obey the church leaders is guilty of insubordination against the divine Master himself." Carried away with his argument, Clement warned that whoever disobeyed the divinely ordained authorities "receives the death penalty"! Pagels goes on to say:

> "[Clement's] *letter marks a dramatic moment in the history of Christianity. For the first time, we find here an argument for dividing the Christian community between 'the clergy' and 'the laity.' The church is to be organized in terms of a strict order of superiors and subordinates*" ("One God, One Bishop: The Politics of Monotheism," *The Gnostic Gospels*, Vintage Books, 1981, p.41).

Sentiments like Clement's could be multiplied, and they highlight how much pull and intimidation leaders had over the common people. We must be aware that a considerable portion of the church's history has been taken up with men who wanted titles, position and authority. As a result of the church being leader-led and leader-dependent for centuries, the only church model people today can relate to is leader-centered. For example, a brochure for the Global Leadership Summit hosted at the Willow Creek Community Church in Illinois said, "Thousands of leaders across North America gather together to hear speakers from all over the world [focus] on helping the church raise up leaders, as well as helping leaders in churches develop their leadership gifts."

The New Testament revelation, however, sees *Christ* as the Leader of His family, not a special class of "clergy." We are so used to looking to human leaders that our sense of Jesus' leadership has been numbed. In Matthew 23, our Lord made it clear that to the degree we elevate humans, His pre-eminence will be diminished.

"They love for people to call them 'Rabbi.' But don't ever let anyone call you 'Rabbi,' for One is your Teacher, and you are all equal...Neither be called 'leaders' because your Leader is One, the Christ."

There are two excellent illustrations of Christ's leadership in the Old Testament, one positive and the other negative. In Exodus 13 we read:

> "Then they set out from Succoth and camped in Etham on the edge of the wilderness. The LORD was going before them in a pillar of cloud by day to lead them on the way, and in a pillar of fire by night to give them light, that they might travel by day and by night. The cloud and the fire were never out of sight."

Here we see the Lord's purpose to guide His people night and day by His Angel, the Lord Jesus Christ. Israel moved when the cloud moved, and remained still when the cloud stopped. The important reality to note here is that *they did not move if the cloud was still, and they did not rest if the cloud moved.* This should be the life-style of the *ekklesia*, to abide in Him and thus be in a posture to let Jesus guide us as the sheep who hear His voice both day and night.

Guidance by the Cloud resulted in some exciting outcomes. As the Red Sea exodus drew near, "the Angel of the Lord, who was leading the people of Israel, moved the cloud around behind them, and it stood between Israel and the Egyptians. And that night, as it turned to a pillar of fire, it gave darkness to the Egyptians but light to Israel. So the Egyptians couldn't find the Israelites!"

At this time of the OT, the people followed a large pillar of fire/smoke. In the NT at Pentecost, each believer had a portion of the flame/Spirit distributed to them. Then, as they come together, each small flame contributed to the current pillar of fire/smoke in discerning the Lord's present direction to rest, move, etc.

In 1 Samuel 8, we see a negative illustration of what occurs when trust is placed in the human realm and not in the 'invisible' Lord:

> They said to him, "You are old, and your sons do not follow your ways; now appoint a king to lead us, such as all the other nations have." But when they said, "Give us a king to lead us," this displeased Samuel; so he prayed to the LORD. And the LORD told him: "Listen to all that the people are saying to you; it is not you they have rejected, but they have rejected me as their king. As they have done from the day I brought them up out of Egypt until this day, forsaking me and serving other gods, so they are doing to you. Now listen to them; but warn them solemnly and let them know what the king who will reign over them will claim as his rights"…But the people refused to listen to Samuel. "No!" they said. "We want a king over us. Then we will be like all the other nations, with a king to lead us and to go out before us and fight our battles."

When Samuel heard all that the people said, he repeated it before the LORD. The LORD answered, "Listen to them and give them a king."

This echoed the tragic picture that unfolded in future church history: a vital, risky and vulnerable trust in the Living Cloud to guide the *ekklesia* was replaced by a power-based human infrastructure. Now, most church members embrace by default this mistaken perspective expressed on Facebook:

> "Someone has to be in charge when a group of people meet. Leader, home owner, maturest Christian whatever title you feel comfortable with. If no one is in charge you end up with a free-for-all" (December 22, 2016).

Probably our biggest challenge is to learn by the Spirit that Jesus is our Pillar of Cloud and Fire. He is fully capable of moving us and stopping us, just as He did the people of Israel. We must understand that Someone is in charge when we gather. He is *Jesus Christ*. If believers trust Him as their Leader, there will be no free-for-alls, but instead beautiful expressions of Him from the Bride.

Every group has leadership, but here is the great divide: is the Lord guiding by the Spirit through all those present, or is the driving force human agendas coming from some sort of "king"? What business do we have worrying about "leaders" when we know so little about Him being our Leader on a practical level?

CHAPTER 16
Family Is "Adam"

Women were removed from the life of the church as the male church hierarchy increased in presence and power from 250AD onwards. The widespread ideology concerning women was reflected in these remarks by Augustine (354-430AD):

"...but separately, as helpmate, the woman herself alone is not the image of God; whereas the man alone is the image of God as fully and completely as when the woman is joined with him."

But Augustine was dead wrong, and his error has perpetuated much untold hurt and misunderstanding in the church. The truth is, the Hebrew word "Adam" includes both men and women. This is brought out clearly in Genesis 5:1-2.

"This is the book of the generations of Adam. In the day that God created Adam, in the likeness of God made he him; male and female created he them, and blessed them, and called their name Adam, in the day when they were created."

In order for the image of God to have full expression, both sexes must be present and functioning. Donald Joy captured this thought well when he said, "We are always impoverished when a single sex group meets, discusses, and makes decisions, since only part of the full-spectrum personhood seems to be present. So where urgent decisions are being made, we surely want both sexes speaking..." (*Bonding*, p. 25).

Of course, Jesus Christ is the fullest and perfect image of God. Adam was a type of the Christ who would come. Thus, Adam had a wife within, and when he fell into a deep sleep, she came forth from his side (*pleura*, Septuagint). Likewise, Christ had a Bride within, and when He fell into the sleep of death, she came forth with water and blood when His side (*pleura*) was pierced (John 19:34). Everything going on in the Adam/Eve narrative was ultimately about Jesus and His Bride, the *ekklesia*.

The *ekklesia*, therefore, is designed by the Lord to be "Adam"—male and female functioning together. This was unveiled on the Day of Pentecost when 120 brothers and sisters spoke in many languages (prophesied), and Peter announced that this was the fulfillment of Joel's words from long ago—"And in the last days it shall be, God declares, that I will pour out my Spirit on all flesh, and your sons and your daughters shall prophesy...even on my male servants and female servants in those days I will pour out my Spirit, and they shall prophesy."

In all the discussion about the "role of women in the church," this passage must not be contradicted. In Messiah's realm both men and women may prophesy without any restrictions. This is relevant for the *ekklesia* as gathered together, for Paul wished that prophecy be central in these times—"you may all prophesy one by one that all may learn and all be encouraged." Both brothers and sisters may exalt the Lord together. In 1 Corinthians 11 Paul echoed what happened on Pentecost—"when any husband or wife prays or prophesies..." Everyone participated in the public gatherings.

There is no need to re-invent the wheel if this is a subject you would like to explore further. Among many helpful treatments, here are five books that cover all the bases from various perspectives.

- Loren Cunningham/David Joel Hamilton, *Why Not Women? A Fresh Look at Scripture on Women in Missions, Ministry and Leadership*, YWAM, 2001.

- Felicity Dale, ed., *The Black Swan Effect: A Response to Gender Hierarchy in the Church*, 2014.

- Philip B. Payne, *Man and Woman, One in Christ: An Exegetical and Theological Study of Paul's Letters*, Zondervan, 2009.

- Ronald Pierce/Rebecca Groothuis, eds., *Discovering Biblical Equaliy: Complementarity without Hierarchy*, IVP, 2005.

- Jon Zens, *What's With Paul & Women? Unlocking the Cultural Background to 1 Timothy 2*, 2010.

Often the issue of women in the church will be stated like this: *is it right for women to stand behind pulpits and preach to a mixed audience?* But in fairness it should really be asked, *is it right for men to stand behind pulpits and preach to a mixed audience?* There is nothing in the New Testament about *anyone* standing behind a "sacred desk" and giving a monologue. The ascent of "the centrality of preaching" pushed the open family gathering described in 1 Corinthians 11 and 14 into oblivion.

The pulpit and preacher epitomize *institutional* Christianity. When you bring Christ's family into an open, caring, loving setting, then gender concerns evaporate. When the brothers and sisters share Christ in humility, then it cannot be about "who's in charge," or the gender of the person speaking. For the full expression of Christ to be a reality, the input of the whole image of God—*male and female*—must be present.

Adam was created as "male and female." Christ by His cross created a "new humanity" which reversed the gender wars, and opened the way for male and female believers to work alongside one another to see Jesus increase on the earth.

CHAPTER 11
Jesus Is Family

The shift from *family* to *institution* is an indisputable historical fact. The early church "was a family…in the apostles' day churches were so small that everyone knew every other and kept a watchful eye on one another" (A.M. Fairbairn, *Studies in Religion & Theology—The Church: In Idea and In History*, The Macmillan Co., 1910, pp. 203, 207). Osiek/Balch noted that as the bishop's power increased, believers' gatherings *"no longer took place in a family environment."*

The loss of the Spirit-led family atmosphere resulted in the exaltation of human traditions devoid of life. In broad strokes this can be illustrated and summarized noting the following contrasts:

- *Humans are made to be relational* vs. Institutions are fundamentally non-relational.

- *Ekklesia gathered in homes as family* vs. Churches meet in special buildings under leaders.

- *Jesus extends hospitality, open space, to His family* vs. Institutional leaders control the sub-culture of the parishioners.

- *Ekklesia is active, pursuing Jesus and working through shared life together* vs. Church is essentially passive, coming to a building, sitting in pews, and watching those up-front do what is deemed important.

- *Family is free to follow the flow of the Spirit, and grow in open space* vs. Church engenders conformity and "institutional forces swallow every attempt at change" (McNiff). Many believers find themselves on a religious treadmill, experiencing what this sister expressed on Facebook:

  > "I've spent the past few years in a spiritual detox. In my lifetime, I've heard more sermons than one could ever possibly need, and I've read more Christian books than anyone should ever read. I've prayer-walked, mission-tripped, youth-grouped, See-Ya-At-The-Poled, and 40-day-fasted. I've kissed dating goodbye, been a missionary, gotten ordained, run a ministry, and been a pastor's wife. And when, at 30-something, my entire life fell apart? None of that mattered. None of it" (January, 2017).

  People can find deliverance from such performance-driven religion in the free family atmosphere, where it is about Jesus instead of doing "things."

- *The safe atmosphere of family opens the door for deepening relationships and for Christ to be expressed in limitless ways* vs. The closed, pre-defined ethos of church stifles relationships and ensures that only one, or a few, will have opportunity for expression.

- *That imperfect people compose the family allows for the body to be real and vulnerable with one another* vs. Church tends to pressure people into keeping up appearances, bearing smiling faces, as if all their ducks are in a row.

- *Family eats together with gladness of heart, feasting on Christ and their fellowship together as one loaf and one cup* vs. Church focuses on coming to a building to hear a sermon, and tacking "Communion" on to the end of a service once a quarter.

- *Family gathers in openness together to enjoy the portion of Christ that each part brings to the table* vs. Church is a "worship service" where 600 ears sit, hear some songs, and listen to one mouth.

- *Family can celebrate Jesus and what He is doing anytime as the Spirit leads* vs. Church tends to use predictable celebrations as occasions for attracting new people or raising money for church programs.

- *In family the draw is Christ in His people; it is small enough where everyone can be known, and relationships in Christ can develop* vs. In church the draw is usually the persona of the pastor, the worship band, or the programs available, not the possibility of vital relationships.

- *In family burdens can be borne because over time the saints know each other; real care, real sensitivity can take place because the love of Christ constrains the relationships* vs. In church too many needs, concerns and heartbreaks fall through the cracks because it is more about the "worship service" than it is about caring for others; often, helping cannot be done directly, but must pass through levels of bureaucracy.

- *All the aspects of healing can be spread out among everyone in the body according to giftedness and relationships; even the loving atmosphere of the body goes a long way to foster healing among the hurting* vs. In church, healing is often not thought of as an ongoing ministry of the body, and if it is, then it is seen as the responsibility of the paid staff to carry it out.

- *To be Spirit-led by Jesus implies a dependent family wanting to hear His voice; His Bride is free to listen and respond to their Leader* vs. In church Jesus is expected to fit into certain prescribed and predictable forms as the people listen to the voice of the pastor and other leaders for direction.

There are so many human hands shaping what is called church that one can hardly doubt that A.W. Tozer's remarks are on target: "If the Holy Spirit was withdrawn from the church today, 95 percent of what we do would go on and no one would know the difference. If the Holy Spirit had been withdrawn from the New Testament *ekklesia* 95 percent of what they did would stop, and everybody would know the difference."

- *In the New Humanity of Christ believers from all ethnic, economic, educational backgrounds, and both genders of all ages, are free to participate in the shared life of Christ together* vs. In most churches, participation is limited to a few; it is not a question just of the women being silenced, for the men are functionally silenced too.

Church historians and New Testament scholars all confess that the early *ekklesia* was marked by a family environment, and driven by the indwelling life of Christ, but that this life was lost in post-apostolic times when the church became a religious institution dominated by male leaders. In 1879 G.A. Jacob pointed out this tendency to skip over the early simplicity and cling to later human traditions:

"Notwithstanding the still generally acknowledged supremacy of Holy Scripture amongst us, the main current of Church opinion on all questions of polity and practice (to say nothing here of doctrines) has for a very considerable time been setting strongly towards the ecclesiastical system of the third and fourth centuries, to the neglect, in this respect, of the New Testament...[The movement] was begun and carried on by men who diligently and perseveringly brought to bear upon the public mind their stores of learning, gathered not from the Apostles, but from the post-apostolic Fathers; not from the divinely taught Church of the New Testament, but from the humanly deteriorated Church of a later time...And all the while there is frequently a profound ignorance of what the Church system at that time really was, and the extent to which it had departed from the simplicity of the apostolic age and truth" (*The Ecclesiastical Polity of the New Testament: A study for the present crisis in the Church of England,* Thomas Whitaker, 1879, pp.20-21, 23).

Does the fact that family became institution concern us? Does the fact that human traditions buried Spirit-simplicity burden our hearts? C.H. Spurgeon in the mid-nineteenth century affirmed the importance of sifting through traditions in order to land on the truth of Christ:

"Happy will the churches be when they shall cast off the yoke of all authority apart from the Scriptures...Away with the commandments of men. Down with the traditions which make void the law of God...A thorough purgation is needed; a root and branch reformation is imperatively necessary."

The Father's purpose was to have a house as a dwelling place. The Son was zealous for His Father's house. The Spirit calls people out of darkness to become a new species, a New Humanity, and the Body of Christ on earth. Is our heart in step with the Godhead's eternal purpose in Christ? Are we tired of playing church, and realizing that the great need is for Spirit-led family? Have we come to long for, as Pete Box put it so well, "face to face community where all have the space to be transparent in their love and pursuit of Jesus the Christ"? (Facebook, January, 2017) Are we beginning to see that "It is quite easy to pivot from what is wrong with one form of church to what is great about another and still miss the primary thing: the life of Christ within you and among you"? (Stephen Mayer, Facebook, February, 2017)

Everett F. Harrison noted that "the homes of the saints [were] where communal meals were enjoyed…A home, as opposed to a public place, would naturally foster a close relationship and encourage the formation of friendships, and impressionable children in the household must have been profoundly influenced as well" ("The Apostolic Church," *Searching Together*, 21:1-4, 1993, pp. 17-18). *This was family!*

It did not last long, and was replaced by an increasing labyrinth of religious machinery. May the Lord stir up our hearts to be totally devoted to the Lord and His purpose to see families, Cities of Refuge, Bethanys and safe places spring up where Jesus can be expressed freely in loving settings!

For Further Reflection

1. Robert Banks, *Going to Church in the First Century*, SeedSowers, 1990, 48 pp.

2. Del Birkey, *The Fall of Patriarchy: It's Broken Legacy Judged by Jesus & the Apostolic House Church Communities*, Fenestra Books, 2005.

3. Craig L. Blomberg, *Contagious Holiness: Jesus' Meals with Sinners*, IVP, 2005.

4. Emil Brunner, *The Misunderstanding of the Church*, Lutterworth, 1952.

5. Michael H. Crosby, *The Dysfunctional Church*, Ave Maria Press, 1991.

6. Thomas Dubay, *Caring: A Biblical Theology of Community*, Dimension Books, 1973.

7. John Eldredge, *Epic*, Thomas Nelson, 2007.

8. Philip F. Esler, editor, *Modelling Early Christianity: Social-Scientific Studies of the New Testament in Its Context*, Routledge, 1995.

9. Gordon Fee, "Cultural Context of Ephesians 5:18-33," https://www. youtube.com/watch?v=6NGhHU0h1RM&list=PL_WBpU8jAuUcG-t0dlPHy5xD82szDzFMM&index=1 (12:24) This is a great overview of the connection between the early household *ekklesias*, their common meals together, and their equality as brothers and sisters.

10. S.D. Gaede, *Belonging: Our Need for Community in Church & Family*, Zondervan, 1985.

11. Ronald F. Hock, *The Social Context of Paul's Ministry: Tentmaking and Apostleship*, Fortress Press, 1980.

12. Donald Joy, *Bonding: Relationships in the Image of God*, 2nd edition, Evangel, 1999.

13. Shaun McNiff, *Art Heals: How Creativity Cures the Soul*, Shambhala Publications, 2004.

14. Henri Nouwen, *Reaching Out: The Three Movements of the Spiritual Life*, Doubleday, 1975.

15. Henri Nouwen, "The Return of the Prodigal Son," 1998, Tape #2, "The Older Son" [cassette]).

16. Julia O'Faolain/Lauro Martines, eds., *Not In God's Image: Women in History from the Greeks to the Victorians*, Harper Torchbooks, 1973, 362 pages.

17. Carolyn Osiek, *A Woman's Place: House Churches in Earliest Christianity*, Fortress Press, 2006.

18. Carolyn Osiek & David L. Balch, *Families in the New Testament: Households & House Churches*, Westminster/John Knox Press, 1997.

19. Milt Rodriguez, *The Community Life of God: Seeing the Godhead as the Model for All Relationships*, The Rebuilders, 2009.

20. Carl R. Rogers, *A Way of Being*, Houghton Mifflin, 1980.

21. Mark Strom, *Reframing Paul: Conversations in Grace & Community*, IVP, 2000.

22. Gerd Theissen, *Social Reality & the Early Christians*, T&T Clark, 1993.

23. Jean Vanier, *From Brokenness to Community*, Paulist Press, 1992.

24. Frank Viola, *From Eternity to Here*, David C. Cook, 2009.

25. Frank Viola, *God's Favorite Place On Earth*, David C. Cook, 2013.

26. Frank Viola, "The Family of God," *Reimagining Church*, David C. Cook, 2007

27. Miriam Weinstein, *The Surprising Power of Family Meals*, Steerforth Press, 2006.

28. Jon Zens, *58 to 0—How Christ Leads Through the One Anothers*, 2013.

29. Jon Zens, YouTube, "The Tucson Videos #7, Jesus Is Building, But Not a Building."

A.W. Tozer's Final Words in 1963

These thoughts were published several days after his death on May 12, 1963. A.W. Tozer's final article strikes a chord with the themes in this book, which are that the body of Christ is designed to function as a family, where Jesus is the Head, and intimate relationships are formed as we listen to and follow Him together. Tozer reveals how rarely this is accomplished in institutional forms of church. These are important points to reflect on as we consider how to move from "church" to *ekklesia*.

Any hard word spoken here against others must in simple honesty return upon my own head. I too have been guilty. This is written with the hope that we all may turn unto the Lord our God and sin no more against Him…

Let me state the cause of my burden. It is this: Jesus Christ has today almost no authority at all among the groups that call themselves by His name. By these I mean not the Roman Catholics nor the liberals, nor the various quasi-Christian cults. I do mean Protestant churches generally, and I include those that protest the loudest that they are in spiritual descent from our Lord and His apostles, namely, the evangelicals…

The present position of Christ in the gospel churches may be likened to that of a king in a limited, constitutional monarchy. The king (sometimes depersonalized by the term "the Crown") is in such a country no more than a traditional rallying point, a pleasant symbol of unity and loyalty much like a flag or a national anthem. He is lauded, feted and supported, but his real authority is small. Nominally he is head over all, but in every crisis someone else makes the decisions. On formal occasions he appears in his royal attire to deliver the tame, colorless speech put into his mouth by the real rulers of the country. The whole thing may be no more than good-natured make-believe, but it is rooted in antiquity, it is a lot of fun and no one wants to give it up.

Among the gospel churches Christ is now in fact little more than a beloved symbol. "All Hail the Power of Jesus' Name" is the church's national anthem and the cross is her official flag, but in the week-by-week services of the church and the day-by-day conduct of her members someone else, not Christ, makes the decisions. Under proper circumstances Christ is allowed to say "Come to me, all you that labor and are heavy laden" or "Let not your heart be troubled," but when the speech is finished someone else takes over. Those in actual authority decide the moral standards of the church, as well as all objectives and all methods employed to achieve them. Because of long and meticulous organization it is now possible for the youngest pastor just out of seminary to have more actual authority in a church than Jesus Christ has.

Not only does Christ have little or no authority; His influence also is becoming less and less. I would not say that He has none, only that it is small and diminishing...The Lordship of Jesus is not quite forgotten among Christians, but it has been relegated to the hymnal where all responsibility toward it may be comfortably discharged in a glow of pleasant religious emotion. Or if it is taught as a theory in the classroom it is rarely applied to practical living. The idea that the Man Christ Jesus has absolute and final authority over the whole church and over all of its members in every detail of their lives is simply not now accepted as true by the rank and file of evangelical Christians.

What we do is this: We accept the Christianity of our group as being identical with that of Christ and His apostles. The beliefs, the practices, the ethics, the activities of our group are equated with the Christianity of the New Testament. Whatever the group thinks or says or does is scriptural, no questions asked. It is assumed that all our Lord expects of us is that we busy ourselves with the activities of the group. In so doing we are keeping the commandments of Christ...

But I suppose I should offer some concrete proof to support my charge that Christ has little or no authority today among the churches. Well, let me put a few questions and let the answers be the evidence.

What church board consults our Lord's words to decide matters under discussion? Let anyone reading this who has had experience on a church board try to recall the times or time when any board member read from the Scriptures to make a point, or when any chairman suggested that the brethren should see what instructions the Lord had for them on a particular question. Board meetings are habitually opened with a formal prayer or "a season of prayer"; after that the Head of the Church is respectfully silent while the real rulers take over. Let anyone who denies this bring forth evidence to refute it. I for one will be glad to hear it.

What Sunday school committee goes to the Word for directions? Do not the members invariably assume that they already know what they are supposed to do and that their only problem is to find effective means to get it done? Plans, rules, "operations" and new methodological techniques absorb all their time and attention. The prayer before the meeting is for divine help to carry out their plans. Apparently the idea that the Lord might have some instructions for them never so much as enters their heads.

Who remembers when a conference chairman brought his Bible to the table with him for the purpose of using it? Minutes, regulations, rules of order, yes. The sacred commandments of the Lord, no. An absolute dichotomy exists between the devotional period and the business session. The first has no relation to the second.

What foreign mission board actually seeks to follow the guidance of the Lord as provided by His Word and His Spirit? They all think they do, but what they do in fact is to assume the scripturalness of their ends and then ask for help to find ways to achieve them. They may pray all night for God to give success to their enterprises, but Christ is desired as their helper, not as their Lord. Human means are devised to achieve ends assumed to be divine. These harden into policy, and thereafter the Lord doesn't even have a vote.

In the conduct of our public worship where is the authority of Christ to be found? The truth is that today the Lord rarely controls a service, and the influence He exerts is very small. We sing of Him and preach about Him, but He must not interfere; we worship our way, and it must be right because we have always done it that way, as have the other churches in our group...

What theological school, from the lowly Bible institute up, could continue to operate if it were to make Christ Lord of its every policy? There may be some, and I hope there are, but I believe I am right when I say that most such schools" to stay in business are forced to adopt procedures which find no justification in the Bible they profess to teach. So we have this strange anomaly: the authority of Christ is ignored in order to maintain a school to teach among other things the authority of Christ.

The causes back of the decline in our Lord's authority are many. I name only two.

One is the power of custom, precedent and tradition within the older religious groups. These like gravitation affect every particle of religious practice within the group, exerting a steady and constant pressure in one direction. Of course that direction is toward conformity to the status quo. Not Christ but custom is lord in this situation. And the same thing has passed over (possibly to a slightly lesser degree) into the other groups such as the full gospel tabernacles, the holiness churches, the pentecostal and fundamental churches and the many independent and undenominational churches found everywhere throughout the North American continent.

The second cause is the revival of intellectualism among the evangelicals. This, if I sense the situation correctly, is not so much a thirst for learning as a desire for a reputation of being learned. Because of it good men who ought to know better are being put in the position of collaborating with the enemy. I'll explain.

Our evangelical faith (which I believe to be the true faith of Christ and His apostles) is being attacked these days from many different directions. In the Western world the enemy has forsworn violence. He comes against us no more with sword and fagot; he now comes smiling, bearing gifts. He raises his eyes to heaven and swears that he too believes in the faith of our fathers, but his real purpose is to destroy that faith, or at least to modify it to such an extent that it is no longer the supernatural thing it once was. He comes in the name of philosophy or psychology or anthropology, and with sweet reasonableness urges us to rethink our historic position, to be less rigid, more tolerant, more broadly understanding...

For the true Christian the one supreme test for the present soundness and ultimate worth of everything religious must be the place our Lord occupies in it. Is He Lord or symbol? Is He in charge of the project or merely one of the crew? Does He decide things or only help to carry out the plans of others? All religious activities, from the simplest act of an individual Christian to the ponderous and expensive operations of a whole denomination, may be proved by the answer to the question, Is Jesus Christ Lord in this act? Whether our works prove to be wood, hay and stubble or gold and silver and precious stones in that great day will depend upon the right answer to that question.

What, then, are we to do? Each one of us must decide, and there are at least three possible choices. One is to rise up in shocked indignation and accuse me of irresponsible reporting. Another is to nod general agreement with what is written here but take comfort in the fact that there are exceptions and we are among the exceptions. The other is to go down in meek humility and confess that we have grieved the Spirit and dishonored our Lord in failing to give Him the place His Father has given Him as Head and Lord of the Church.

Either the first or the second will but confirm the wrong. The third if carried out to its conclusion can remove the curse. The decision lies with us.

[The whole of his remarks in 1963 can be found at http://www.awtozerclassics. com/articles/article/4938678/86408.htm]

For more information about Jon Zens
or to contact him for speaking engagements,
please visit *www.SearchingTogether.org*

Many voices. One message.

Quoir is a boutique publishing company
with a single message: Christ is all.
Our books explore both His
cosmic nature and corporate expression.

For more information, please visit
www.quoir.com

CPSIA information can be obtained
at www.ICGtesting.com
Printed in the USA
FSOW03n0316120517
34046FS

9 781938 480232